**Also by Deanna Brann, Ph.D.**

RELUCTANTLY RELATED:
*Secrets to Getting Along with Your*
*Mother-in-Law or Daughter-in-Law*

MOTHERS-IN-LAW & DAUGHTERS-IN-LAW
SAY THE DARNDEST THINGS

**Visit www.DrDeannaBrann.com**

# Reluctantly Related Revisited

### Breaking Free of the Mother-in-Law/Daughter-in-Law Conflict

## Deanna Brann, Ph.D.

### YOUR IN-LAW SURVIVAL GUIDE

**Illustrations by Donald Hoenig**

AMBERGRIS

*Reluctantly Related Revisited: Breaking Free of the
Mother-in-Law/Daughter-in-Law Conflict*

Copyright @ 2016 by Deanna Brann, Ph.D.
Illustrations by Donald Hoenig

Published by

*a* Ambergris Publishing
Knoxville, TN
**AMBERGRIS**

ISBN: 978-0-9888100-2-0
eISBN: 978-0-9888100-3-7

Printed in the United States of America

Cover and interior design by GKS Creative
Author Photo by Christian Lange

All stories and examples are not representative of any
one individual or any one particular person's experience,
but rather they are a composite of like personalities,
relationships, and situations.

Library of Congress Control Number:  2016900718

*This book is dedicated to the women who experience pain and fragility in their in-law relationships—and to the men who love them.*

# Acknowledgments

Researching this book was a journey with many unexpected twists and turns. I started out thinking I was writing a book on the other in-laws in one's life, when in fact, the research led me to write another book about the MIL/DIL relationship with the addition of the other in-laws (and more). A truly amazing ride!

I want to thank the following people for their invaluable assistance:

All the in-laws—mothers-in-law, fathers-in-law, daughters-in-law, sons-in-law, sisters-in-law, and brothers-in-law—who shared their stories with me. Your disclosure took courage and trust, and I am forever grateful that you entrusted me with a part of your life that—positively or negatively—has impacted you so much.

My husband, Roger Monforton, whose love and support made this process so much easier. As always, you helped me sort through and clarify my thoughts when they were not clear, as well as helped me make sense of things when I couldn't on my own. Knowing your only agenda has been to help me succeed in whatever I choose to do has made it easier to trust this process. You also provided humor when I found myself so mired in the process that I struggled to find my way out.

Elise Clodfelter, my oldest granddaughter, who helped me to smooth out the rough drafts and refine many of the illustrative designs for the book. Throughout this process, your insight and editorial abilities were invaluable. Working with you on this project has given me a chance to see you as more than my granddaughter. It has given me a chance to see you as a young woman in your own right. It's been a delight to discuss, explain, and laugh with you along the way. Sharing the many different psychological components, characteristics, and processes that go into people's behavior and the various aspects that have been included in this book have given me a new perspective into the depth of your understanding of human nature.

Sharon Hall, whose friendship I will forever cherish. Your continued love and support has been exactly what I've needed as life's detours have crept in and, at times, taken priority. You've been instrumental in helping me shift my perspective when it was needed and showing me that when things happen that I don't understand, the meaning and clarity often comes down the road. You are truly a sage.

Katy Koontz, my editor who worked her magic as much in this book as she did in the first one. Your gift for understanding my voice and making my concepts and thoughts clearer has made this book even better than the first. Having our relationship evolve into a friendship has been one of the joys of this process.

Don Hoenig, who has made my words and concepts come alive through the book's illustrations. It has been a pleasure continuing to work through the process of vague concept to actual picture—not always easy, but always gratifying. Your easy-going nature and sense of humor has made this illustrative journey a process to remember. Thank you for that!

Susan Morales, a dear friend whose insight and wisdom have given me perspective when I've needed it. Talking through some of the concepts and processes with me opened my eyes in ways I could not have achieved alone. You have a unique way of looking at behavior that is both astute and refreshing.

Bethany Brown of The Cadence Group, who has made packaging and marketing this book such an easy journey. Working with you has restored my faith in what has often been known as the painful side of authorship. Your eye for detail as well as your extensive experience in the publishing world has been invaluable.

# Contents

# CHAPTER 1

# Mired in Misery

*Family members have different ideas and expectations about how they should act toward each other— especially after grown children marry. The friction that results can be frustrating for everyone.*

CHANCES ARE, you've picked up this book because there's some strain or tension in your relationship between you and your in-law—whether the trouble is with your mother-in-law (MIL) or with your daughter-in-law (DIL). So let me reassure you right from the start that there's hope. In fact, there's an excellent chance you can make huge strides to repair and improve the relationship. Will it be easy? Well, that depends—on how bad things are and on how invested you are in working to change them.

Of course, I have no real magic wand to offer, and yet many of the concepts, ideas, and techniques I will share in this book may well work like magic for many readers. The biggest factor in whether the advice and guidance I offer will make a difference or not is *you*—how ready you are to make some changes *yourself.*

Now hold on a second, *I'm not at all saying you're to blame.* You're not necessarily the one who is most at fault. The thing is, looking at the problem in that sort of two-dimensional I'm-right-and-she-is-wrong way is only stoking the fire. It isn't offering you a way out, even if you *are* 100 percent right. What I'm about to offer you is the opportunity to step back and take a three-dimensional look at what's going on, getting underneath it and peering over the top of it, and taking a good look at it from several different angles. What you will see when you do this will almost definitely surprise you.

And then, with some out-of-the box solutions you'll read about for handling what you've become convinced is impossible to handle, you'll be able to much more easily see a very workable way out (maybe with one or two small course corrections along the way)—without any bloodshed, without burning any bridges, and without having a nervous breakdown (or filing for divorce) in the process. In fact, you might even be able to do it all keeping your sense of humor perfectly intact. (At least, that's my goal.)

But first, let's look at several different scenarios in this chapter and the next that will describe in detail the kind of dynamic that's been driving you (and your spouse) up the wall. If you recognize yourself and your in-law in any of these stories, hold on. Help's coming!

## Janet, Charlene, and Dan

Charlene stormed out of the room, her MIL's voice still chiding her as she slipped into the study and shut the door. She couldn't take one more minute in the same room with Janet. This was the last straw. As she sat in the study staring out the window with her toddler in her arms, Charlene kept thinking over and over, *What right does she have to tell me what to do with my own child? And then to try and take her out of my arms while I'm comforting her! Not this time!* Charlene could hear Janet in the next room, huffing and sighing while mumbling under her breath. But she didn't care. She was not about to let her MIL bulldoze her into compromising what she *knew* to be right for her and *her* baby.

This is not the first time Charlene has had issues with Janet, and she is sure it won't be the last. Charlene and her husband Dan have tried numerous times to rein his mother in, but things always seem to get worse. Janet's constant phone calls and text messages create feelings of guilt, self-doubt, frustration, anger, and overall weariness in both Dan and Charlene. What's more, Janet's constant barrage of intrusive behavior has strained the couple's marriage. Dan and Charlene often disagree with how the other deals with or reacts to Janet's behavior, which in turn causes them to get angry and argue with one another.

It seems that no matter how often they talk about his mother and what to do about her antics, nothing seems to change. They both feel helpless in these situations, and what's more, Dan feels an overwhelming amount of guilt—not only guilt that his mother is creating so much havoc in their lives, but also guilt for how hurt and sad his mother appears whenever he tries to set boundaries with her. Everyone else in the family seems so normal, showing respect for what Charlene and Dan want for *their* family, so neither Dan nor Charlene has any idea why things are so difficult with Janet.

The tensions with Janet started long before Charlene and Dan got married. Janet wanted to control everything in their lives, including when the wedding was going to be, where it was going to be, where they were going to live, and how often they spent time with her. There seemed to be no end to the control Janet wanted to exert. Charlene initially tried to be understanding and patient with her MIL, thinking Janet's antics were her way of dealing with the fact that her son was transitioning from being single to being married. But their wedding was three years ago, and Janet's behavior only got worse, particularly since their daughter was born a little over a year ago.

This particular visit from Janet was not something Dan or Charlene really wanted—they'd felt obligated as a last resort. Janet had been saying to them every chance she got, "Why don't you ever come visit us? It's been months since you've been here. I just want to spend some time with my grandbaby. You're depriving Charlotte of a chance to get to know her Gama."

Finally, after listening to this for the umpteenth time, Dan said to his mother, "Look, Mom, it's not easy for us to travel right now. Charlotte is still pretty young; the car ride is horrendous for everyone and it takes a lot out of us. It's just not something we want to do right now."

Initially there was silence, followed by an outburst of sobbing. Janet was uncontrollable. Dan felt horrible. He hated it when his mother cried, and this time was worse than usual. "Mom, why are you crying?" Dan asked with a mixture of apprehension and irritation in his voice. Janet tried to talk a little bit, but her sobbing made it impossible. At this point, he just wanted—*needed*—her to get herself under control. "Just stop crying," Dan continued. "We'll figure something out."

After what seemed like a lifetime, Dan said as calmly and in as upbeat a voice as he could muster, "Anyway, when was the last time you came here? If I remember, you've been here only once, and that was when we were first married. Why don't you visit us? After all, it's easier for you to make the trip here than it is for us to come there." As soon as he said it, he wished he hadn't. *What was he going to do with her here? What was Charlene going to do with her?*

As soon as the words were out of Dan's mouth, Janet stopped crying. "Are you sure? Well...I could come in a few weeks. Let me look at the calendar, and I will email you dates that will work for me." Janet's whole mood had changed. Dan just sighed, glad she had stopped crying, but angry with himself for falling for her manipulative behavior *again*.

Dan knew he was going to have to talk to Charlene soon because he *really* needed her help with this. He just hoped she'd understand. He was restless and uneasy at the thought of bringing up a possible visit from his mother, but he knew he had to do it. Since there really was no *good* time for this, with trepidation he soon approached Charlene.

"I talked to my mom the other day," he began. "She started in again about the fact that we haven't visited her in ages. I told her how hard it was for us to do that, and then she started with her crying and sobbing thing. I just couldn't take it. So I said, 'Why don't you come here? It would be easier for you to come here than for us to go there.' Now don't get mad, Char—I know I shouldn't have said that, and I'm sorry, but I didn't know what else to do. You know how she is!"

Yes, Charlene knew how her MIL could be. She also knew how her husband could be. He seemed to have the worst time standing up to his mother. *She really knows how to push his buttons,* she thought. *And he falls for it every time!* One of the qualities Charlene loves about

Dan is how kind and compassionate he is. But sometimes he goes too far—at least when it comes to his mother. He just can't seem to stand up to her, and when he does, she can turn him around within seconds. It is maddening! It's as though Dan knows what his mother is doing, but he can't stop himself.

Charlene was beside herself. She felt bad for her husband because she knew how hard it was for him to push back with his mother, but she also didn't want him to think she was fine with what he did. "Dan," she said with an edge to her voice, "I can't believe you invited her here. I know how your mom can push your buttons, but having her come *here*? I mean, what are we going to *do* with her? She's going to want to take over *everything*. And we'll have to deal with her snide remarks—*all day long!*"

Charlene was on a roll. She had so many pent up feelings about Janet that she couldn't stop even if she wanted to—and at this moment, she didn't want to. "She's going to criticize *everything*—what I'm doing with Charlotte, how I've decorated the house, the size of the baby's bedroom, why I haven't lost my baby weight." Charlene barely took a breath. Her panic was escalating. "She's going to ask where the dishes are that she gave us and why we don't use them, why we keep the house so cold, why we let Charlotte play with certain things, why we feed Charlotte this or that, and it will go on and on the whole time she is here. And the *worst* part of it, Dan, is that you don't have to hear hardly any of this because you're at work all day."

Dan felt horrible. He knew Charlene was right. He had really messed up this time. "I know, I know. But I didn't know what else to do. The words just seemed to come out of my mouth before I had a chance to think. I'm really sorry. I'll tell you what—let's limit her visit to three days. I'll take off work while she's here so you don't have to be the only one dealing with her all day."

Charlene actually felt a bit better after venting, but she knew her venting hadn't really solved the problem. All the things she had just complained about to Dan were things that happened *any* time she was around Janet. And the fact remained that Janet was still coming to visit.

"All right," Charlene sighed, resigning herself to the fact that what was done was done. "Let's think about what we can do while she is here to make life easier for *us*. But Dan, you *have* to deal with how your mom is able to manipulate you. This can't go on…and you know it's only going to get worse now that Charlotte is here. It's not fair to me. And I can't stand to see how tormented you are after one of those conversations with her. So promise me, okay?" Dan knew Charlene was right. He didn't like how he handled things with his mother either, but he wasn't really sure what he could do differently that would work.

Dan and his mother went around and around about dates and times. Janet wanted to come for a week and a half, but Dan stood firm on three days. Janet tried everything to get her way—including crying, sounding angry, and pouting—but she eventually agreed to the three-day visit. Both Dan and Charlene felt good that *finally* they were doing things on *their* terms.

Then the day of the visit arrived. Janet was coming in on a late-morning flight and Dan was picking her up at the airport. She no sooner got in the car than she said to Dan, "I hope Charlene's not going to be one of those mothers who watches *everything* I do with the baby. They always act as though the grandmother knows nothing about being a parent. Do they forget that we had children too?"

"Mom, why are you saying that?" Dan asked. "You know Charlene isn't like that."

"Well, I don't know that! I haven't been around her much since Charlotte was born, or have you forgotten? It seems that since Charlotte came, you both stay away from us as much as possible. I guess we're just not good enough."

"Mom, we're done here, okay?" Dan responded, sounding more than a little irritated. "No more talk about Charlene, how we handle Charlotte, or what we do or don't do that you don't like." They rode the rest of the way in silence. Dan was seething. He just couldn't believe his mother had started in on her verbal barrage before they had even arrived at the house. This was going to be a *long* weekend!

When Janet walked in the front door, she sat her bags down and without even saying hello to Charlene asked, "Where's Charlotte? Her Gama's here." Charlene shook her head, but decided she was not going to let this bother her.

"Janet, it's great to see you!" she said, ignoring her MIL's rude behavior. "How was your flight?"

Janet waved Charlene off as she looked around for Charlotte, mumbling, "Cold, but uneventful."

Things didn't get much better as the afternoon progressed. Janet's "suggestions" seemed to go on endlessly: "It is so cold in here! Charlotte's feet are turning blue. Why don't you have socks on her?" "Here let me take her. This is what I used to do with Danny when he was a baby and he loved it!" and "You know it would be easier for you if you put things away as you go. Your house would stay so much neater."

Although Dan and Charlene had worked out a plan where they each allowed for personal downtime away from Janet, both were feeling the stress of needing to constantly deflect, dodge, and weave around Janet's remarks, not to mention protect their daughter's personal space. They were exhausted, but by the time the weekend was almost over, they could finally see the light at the end of the tunnel. Janet would be going home soon.

Late in the day, Charlene and Janet were in the sunroom when Charlotte came toddling over to her mother. She was upset, crying. It was hard for her to talk in between her sobs, but eventually she was able to say that she had been scratched while playing with the cat. She was bleeding a bit, but nothing serious. As Charlene was trying to tend to her daughter's wounds—physical as well as emotional—Janet jumped in, yelling at Charlene.

"Why do you keep that darn cat?" she screeched. "It's nothing but a menace around poor Charlotte. Here, let me take her. She needs her Gama right now. And you need to do something about that cat!" As Charlotte finished putting a dab of first-aid cream on her daughter's small cut, ignoring Janet's outburst, her MIL blurted out, "I don't think putting that stuff on her wound is going to help. The more you coddle her the more she is going to cry. Put her down. I know just the thing that will work...."

As Janet kept going on and on, getting more demanding with every word, it just became too much for her DIL to take. Charlene got up and stormed out of the room, carrying a puzzled Charlotte and heading for the study—leaving Janet in midsentence.

### Sharon, Jenna, and Scott

"Mom, I don't know why it always has to be about you. You make it so hard for us to want to be around you!" Scott shouted into the phone, frustrated that he seemed to have the same conversation with his mother again and again. *Why can't she get that we have other priorities besides just her?* he thought, fuming.

Sharon, Scott's mother, was stunned. *Why is this happening to me?* she kept asking herself as she got off the phone with her son. *He never used to treat me like this. I can't understand why he is acting this way. He's so distant now. Ever since he's been with Jenna....*

Sharon and her son Scott had been close throughout his life. In fact, their whole family was close. Even when he was in college, Scott would call at least once a week, sometimes twice. Of course, he didn't necessarily talk to Sharon every time; he would often call to talk to his brother or dad, yet she could count on talking to him at least one of those times.

Scott had also always come home for the holidays. Even if he happened to be involved with someone, he would either come alone or bring his girlfriend with him. Sharon always tried to make sure whomever he brought home felt welcomed. In fact, Sharon remembers their home being the place where all of Scott's friends would gather. It was like their home away from home. And they always called her "Mom."

However, ever since he started dating Jenna, Scott's behavior was different. In fact, he had become rather secretive. For the longest time he didn't share the fact that he was seeing her with anyone in the family. It wasn't until they were almost engaged that Scott introduced his family to Jenna. This caught everyone—especially Sharon—by surprise. She felt hurt because Scott had been keeping his relationship such a secret and she didn't understand why.

At one point she actually brought it up with him. "Scott, why didn't you tell us about Jenna before now?" she asked. "This is so unlike you. You've always been so open with me, and with all of us, and now…well, I just don't understand."

Scott felt pushed. He wasn't quite sure what to say, and he was annoyed at his mother for asking. It felt like prying to him, intrusive in a way. He felt like pushing back, but he didn't. He quickly thought of something to say to appease her, without turning the situation into some big drama.

"Mom, I don't know," he answered. "I guess I didn't think about it. My relationship with Jenna just sort of happened, and then before we knew it we were caught up in it. I wasn't intentionally trying to keep it from you."

Sharon didn't really believe what her son was saying, but she could tell from his voice that he didn't want to talk about it. She didn't like where this conversation was going, and she didn't want to make things worse so she decided to let it go. Jenna was going to be part of the family, and Sharon made up her mind to embrace her. Sharon's resolve was to view this new situation as gaining a daughter instead of losing—or partially losing—a son.

Sharon made every effort to welcome Jenna into the family. And though she understood the young couple's need to have their own time, she also wanted Scott and Jenna to know she was there for them in any way they might need. Jenna enjoyed Scott's parents and brother when she first met them. Everyone was warm, friendly, and more than willing to accept her into their family. Even though she and Scott did not see much of them while they were dating, it felt as though she was still able to build a fairly good relationship with them. But after some time, the situation felt as though something had inexplicably changed.

Scott and Jenna's lives moved on—they got engaged, got married, and moved into a new house. Sharon tried hard to keep in contact with them on a regular basis, talking with Jenna as much as with Scott. Initially Jenna was friendly, yet to Sharon, Jenna also felt a little distant—pleasant, but a bit detached. And although that hurt Sharon, she chalked it up to Jenna's busy schedule with work, home, activities, and so on. As time went on, though, Jenna seemed to pick up the phone only sporadically, and when she did it was as though she was always in a hurry to get off.

For Jenna, though, Sharon's need to be involved was a bit hard to take. Sharon seemed to have opinions about their engagement party, the wedding guest list, and her role in the wedding planning. She also wanted to help the couple move in to their new home. Jenna appreciated Sharon's helpfulness, but she had to admit that dealing with her MIL was at times exhausting, if not altogether overwhelming.

Sharon seemed to have better luck talking to Scott. She continued to talk with him on a weekly basis, even after he and Jenna were married. The conversations did change some, with his sharing less about what was going on in their lives. Nevertheless, Sharon enjoyed the time talking with her son—even if it was by phone. After a while, she noticed their calls were becoming shorter and shorter, with less information. And Scott seemed to have developed a bit of an edge to his voice.

Several times Scott would say to her, "Look, Mom, I can't talk right now. I'll have to call you back." But he rarely did. Although this concerned Sharon, she tried hard to not let her fears get the best of her. After all, they'd always been so close, right? And she was continuing to show interest in their lives and to offer help when needed. Surely this wasn't about *her*.

Then one day, Sharon realized it had been a while since she'd talked to Scott. She thought the last conversation she had with him went well, and even though his phone calls had become less frequent, it still seemed odd to her that she hadn't heard from him in so long. She texted him a few times, but he didn't respond. So she decided to call him and maybe invite him and Jenna over for dinner. She called. No answer. She left a voicemail. Days went by and she heard nothing from him—no voicemail, no text—nothing.

Sharon wasn't sure how she felt—angry, anxious, frustrated? Maybe all three. All she wanted was to spend some time with her son and his wife, maybe have them over for dinner, but they couldn't even return a phone call! *What was up with that?* She was tired of reaching out to Scott and Jenna and getting nothing back. And even when they *did* respond, it was as though she was bothering them.

Sharon felt her son was no longer the person he used to be. He didn't seem happy. He appeared rushed all the time, as though he couldn't catch his breath, always making excuses for not spending time with the family. It seemed to Sharon he was acting a bit withdrawn and isolating himself. And Jenna rarely talked to her at all now. It was as though her DIL didn't want anything to do with his side of the family anymore.

All Sharon could think was, *He never used to be like this. Something must be going on. It's as though Jenna doesn't like him talking to me. Whenever I do talk with him he is in the car on his way home from work—he's never at home. And on top of it all, he sounds irritated, tense, and even angry.* Sharon felt bad for Scott. She just knew something was wrong and he wasn't sharing whatever it was with those who loved him. Although she couldn't put her finger on anything specific with Jenna, she felt her DIL was at the root of whatever was going on.

Her leaving messages without getting a response from them went on for months on end, but Sharon didn't want to stop reaching out to Scott, even though she had pretty much given up trying with Jenna. She missed her son and wanted the family to feel whole again. She wasn't sure what to do. Then, she remembered that Scott's birthday was coming up in a few weeks, so she decided to invite them for a barbeque at the lake house to celebrate. It would be great!

After leaving several messages, Sharon finally got Scott to call her back. She decided to make their conversation short and to the point so that he would appreciate the fact that she was not trying to take time away from whatever he was doing. Since the last conversation had been somewhat tense, almost on the verge of being uncomfortable, Sharon planned to make this one as upbeat as she could.

"Hi, Scott!" she started. "I was thinking about your birthday and thought it would be great if you and Jenna came up to the lake house with us either this coming weekend or the next to celebrate. You know, a birthday weekend."

"Mom, I really don't know if that will work for us," Scott answered. "We have a lot going on, and I think Jenna was planning something." Sharon felt hurt and frustrated. She really didn't think she was asking that much of them.

"For *both* weekends?" she asked, trying to keep her voice calm, but unable to prevent it from getting edgy, maybe even somewhat sharp. "I just want to try to spend some time with you. You know, we rarely get to see you anymore. Your father was hoping the two of you could do some fishing while we were there. You guys always enjoyed that." Now Scott was annoyed. He wasn't sure what else he could say that would make the situation any clearer to his mother.

"Mom, I don't know what you want. I've told you it doesn't look like it will work for us," he said, his voice escalating. Now Sharon was getting mad.

"I *want* to spend time with my son! Is that such a horrible thing?" she responded, her voice getting louder and higher with each word. "We try hard to give you and Jenna your space, but you never reach out to us about getting together. And then when we reach out to you, you act as though we are being unreasonable. That doesn't seem very fair, Scott. What are we supposed to do—accept the fact that we will *never* see you?"

"Now *you're* being unfair!" Scott shouted into the phone. "You act as though we are deliberately staying away from you. We're not. We *do* have our own lives, you know. Did you ever think about that?" His outburst brought his mother close to tears.

"I just didn't think we were asking that much of you. We are still your family, Scott," Sharon said, her voice shaking.

Silence. After a few *very long* seconds Sharon tentatively asked, "Scott, are you there?" Again, there was a long, deafening pause. Finally Scott responded. The accusation he shouted into the phone was something Sharon never imagined she'd ever hear from her son.

# CHAPTER 2

# Where Do We End and I Begin?

*The key to being close with family—in a healthy way—is understanding the balance between closeness and autonomy.*

DID YOU RECOGNIZE YOURSELF or your in-law in either of the two stories from the last chapter? At the very least, you probably identified with the feeling of hopelessness that many of the different people felt in dealing with their in-laws (and even their spouses). In this chapter, I'm going to share two more stories with you—these illustrating the problems people can have when families get a little *too* close.

## Andrea, Eric, and Judy

*When is it ever going to be* our *turn?* Judy wondered as she hung up the phone with her son Eric. Feeling raw with emotion, she began to cry, disheartened that her DIL Andrea always seems to be running the whole show—at least when it comes to their family. This was not the first time Judy and her husband have had to take a back seat to their DIL's family. In fact, it seems as though they are always taking a back seat to them.

Judy and her husband now live only about twenty minutes from Eric and Andrea. When she heard that her son and his wife were moving back home, near where they both grew up, Judy couldn't wait. She found herself imaging how things would be. *Finally, we will get to be more of a family,* she'd thought. *And spending time with the two grandkids will be so much easier.*

Judy knew that Andrea's parents lived close by as well, and she thought it would finally be more balanced having both sets of grandparents available to watch the children and be a bigger part of their lives. Although she and Andrea's mother were not particularly close, she felt they could forge some kind of relationship, especially if it was for the sake of the family. From Judy's perspective, Andrea's mother Cindy came across as extremely nice—almost too nice. When they had been around one another in the past, Cindy's smiles, winks, and cajoling seemed to have an undercurrent of edginess to them. There wasn't anything Judy could point to specifically and say, "See? Cindy is undermining me," or "Cindy is trying to control Eric and Andrea," but she always seemed to feel an undercurrent of that nonetheless.

After Eric and Andrea had been back for about six months, Judy could count on one hand the number of times that she and her husband had seen them or the grandkids. Judy has done her best to brush it aside, but sometimes her thoughts get the better of her. *I feel like I've lost my son and my grandkids, and there seems to be nothing I can do,* she thought. *They are always doing things with her family! I can't compete with that, and Eric won't fight for us at all. I just don't understand....*

Andrea was the one who wanted to move back closer to family, although Eric didn't really mind. Andrea had missed her family, and even though her mother visited frequently, Andrea thought it would be great to be able to have them more involved with the grandkids. She talked to her mother almost every day, if not every day, and the chance to spend time with her had been just what Andrea dreamed it would be.

Andrea has found herself confiding more and more in her mother, because her mother seems to be able to relate to a lot of the problems or issues Andrea is experiencing at this point in her life. Her mother's availability to watch the children makes it easy for Andrea as well.

It isn't that Andrea *never* asks her MIL to watch the grandkids, she simply prefers her mother to his because it seems easier. And if Andrea is honest with herself, she has to admit she is obviously more comfortable with her own mother. Andrea doesn't have anything against her MIL. Judy is nice enough. Andrea just doesn't feel they have that much in common and it seems to her that they really don't have much of a relationship with one another.

Eric was happy enough moving back to be close to family, although that probably wouldn't have been his first choice of places to live. He knew Andrea missed her family, and if being closer to them made her happy, he was all for it. At first, he was fine being around her family for the most part, since they treated him as one of their own. However, now, at times, he gets this sense that he's competing with them—and not just for Andrea's time. He almost feels as though his wife's parents—and her mother in particular—have become part of *his and Andrea's* marriage. Eric no longer feels as though it's just him and Andrea. Eric feels as though it's become him, Andrea, *and her mother*!

Eric remembered one specific incident that seemed to drive this feeling home. On that evening, Andrea's mother was over chatting with Eric while she waited for Andrea to return from work. As they talked, she made what seemed to Eric like a strange comment that made it clear she assumed that he and Andrea needed a new car. He didn't think much of it at first, but as the conversation went on, he began wondering about it. *Why would she make a comment about our needing a new car?* he thought. *She said it as if she knew something that I might not know—or at least she acted as though she knew more than she was saying.* Either way, Eric felt a bit uncomfortable.

He and Andrea had been going around and around about wanting versus needing a new car. Andrea had shared all the reasons why she felt it was not just a want, but truly a need. Eric, on the other hand, thought they should wait a while before getting a new car. He didn't feel they could swing it financially, especially since a new car payment would substantially increase their budget. They seemed to be getting nowhere with their discussion—neither one was able to sway the other. They were at an impasse.

The comments by Andrea's mother, as well as the overall sense that she knew something he didn't (or something he *should*), left Eric with an eerie feeling of subterfuge or being "managed." After Andrea's mother left that evening, Eric decided to get to the bottom of things. He did not like how he felt or what he thought was going on.

"Andrea, your mom made some comments to me about our *needing* a car," he said to his wife once they were alone. "Why would she say something like that?"

"How should I know?" Andrea responded, although more tentatively than she might normally have answered.

"What do you mean, 'How should I know?'" Eric retorted. "Did you say something to her about the fact that we've been arguing over whether or not to get a new car?"

Andrea knew this was not going to go well, but she didn't think she had done anything *really* wrong. *After all,* she thought, *Eric knows I share things with my mom, and he never seemed to mind before.* "Well, yes, I did say something to my mom," she said sheepishly. Then moving into a more defensive, almost defiant posture, she added, "You know I talk to her about things. I didn't realize you would be so touchy about this, or I never would have said anything!"

Eric was furious. He was tired of "their" business also being her mother's business, and this was not the first fight they'd had about her mother being in their affairs. But he also knew if he said anything more they would end up in another *huge* fight. Afraid he might say something he'd later regret, he decided it was best for him to say nothing more. Instead, he shook his head and stormed out of the room. *Better to just let things cool off for a while,* he thought as he went out the door.

*Why is he so upset?* Andrea wondered to herself. *He's making such a big deal about this. It's not like I share* everything *with my mom. He should be glad I talk with her. If I didn't, he'd have to deal with* all *of my feelings.*

Eric and Andrea kept their distance from one another for the next several hours. By that evening, they cautiously felt each other out to get a read on where the other person was. Neither said anything about what had happened earlier in the day, nor did either of them want to deal with it now. They both just wanted things to go back to normal, and with some time, that appeared to be the case.

Eric wanted to put his memory of this incident as far back in his mind as possible so that they could go back to a more normal place. Andrea also wanted to move on from the discomfort she felt concerning Eric's comments about her mother. Both buried their feelings as best they could.

With the weekend in just a few days and things appearing to have calmed down between her and Eric, Andrea made plans for them to go to her parents' cabin in the mountains. Andrea's sister was going to be there with her family, as well as her parents. Although they didn't do it every weekend, going to the cabin with her family seemed to have become somewhat of a weekend ritual since summer began. Andrea loved it, and even though Eric didn't make it every time due to work, she knew Eric and the kids enjoyed it as well.

In the meantime, Judy had been trying to get ahold of Andrea for a few days now, yet every time she called, she got her DIL's voicemail. She had left a few messages, asking Andrea to call her back, but Andrea never did. Judy wanted to have them over for a barbeque that coming weekend and thought if she called early enough in the week, she could catch them before they had a chance to make plans. In the past, Judy had tried to make plans more than a week in advance, but Andrea made a point of telling her they couldn't commit that far ahead. Frustrated with her DIL for not returning her phone calls, Judy decided to call her son.

"Eric, I've tried to get a hold of Andrea, but she doesn't seem to be returning my calls," Judy said. "I'm not sure what is going on, but the reason I was calling is we wanted to see if you, Andrea, and the kids could come over sometime this coming weekend for a barbeque. We haven't seen you in a while, and we thought it would give us all a chance to catch up on what everyone has been up to. And we'd really love to see the grandkids!"

Since he and Andrea had not talked about the upcoming weekend, Eric wasn't sure if they already had plans. And although that didn't always mean that Andrea hadn't planned something for them without telling him, he was fine seeing if they could get together with his side of the family. "Sure, Mom, let me check with Andrea just to make sure we don't have anything planned," Eric said. "I'll call you tomorrow and let you know."

For the first time in a long time, Judy was hopeful that maybe they would finally get to see Eric and Andrea without a tug-of-war from her DIL's side of the family. But she was well aware that until the plans were confirmed, anything could happen. And so she waited.

During dinner that night, Eric approached Andrea with the possibility of going to his parents' house for a barbeque. "My mom called today and invited us over sometime this weekend for a barbeque," he said to his wife. "I told her I didn't think we had anything planned, but that I'd check with you first. So what do you think?"

Andrea took a deep breath and let out a heavy sigh. "Well," she said, "I talked to my mom already about going to the cabin. My sister and her family will be there. My parents will be there, too. I'd really like to go to the cabin."

"But we have been there a lot this summer already," Eric replied. "Why can't we go to my parents' for one afternoon this weekend, and then if you still want to go to the cabin afterward, we can do that?"

"I *really* don't feel like going to your parents' house," Andrea answered with an edgy tone.

"That's not a reason, Andrea," Eric said, now clearly annoyed. "One afternoon won't kill you. After all, we see your family all the time."

"I know," Andrea fought back, shaking her head as she rolled her eyes. "But I'm more comfortable with my family, and I know you enjoy being around them, too. And the kids love playing with their cousins. There's nothing for the kids to do at your parents' house." She waited a few seconds and then added, "Anyway, I already said something to my mom. She's expecting us."

Eric did not want to have another argument with Andrea. One fight a week was more than enough for him. He did, however, want to make sure he got his point across. "All right, we'll go to the cabin this weekend," he said. "But you have to *promise* me that we will not go there again until we've spent some time with *my* family." Begrudgingly Andrea agreed, but she didn't commit to any particular weekend.

When Eric told his mother about their plans to go to the cabin for the weekend, Judy tried hard not to show her agitation and disappointment, and more importantly, her anger. "I don't understand, Eric," she said in a controlled tone. "We haven't seen you guys in so long and *her* parents see you all the time. I just thought maybe we would get a turn once in a while."

As soon as she said those words, she knew she'd made a mistake. She didn't want to put Eric in the middle, she just didn't know what else to do. "Eric, I'm sorry," she said quickly. "I don't want to put you in the middle, really. Will you think about maybe doing something with us the following weekend, then? Or, the weekend after?"

Eric felt a twinge of guilt and sadness. He knew his mother was trying really hard to be as respectful of them as possible. And he appreciated her for it. "Sure, Mom, let me look at the calendar and talk with Andrea," he said. "I promise we will get together one of those weekends."

Judy felt a little bit of relief, but mostly she felt dejected. As she got off the phone with Eric, her emotional floodgates opened up.

### Kate, Adam, and Teresa

Teresa was at a loss to understand what had just happened at her son and DIL Kate's house while she was there. Close to tears, she shared her story with her closest friend, hoping that maybe she could help her make sense of things. "I thought everything was fine," she explained, "but all of a sudden, out of the blue, Kate let me know—in no uncertain terms, mind you—that I had made a *huge* mess of things." Teresa struggled to find the right words to describe the events that happened next. "It was my day to watch the baby, and I had just finished cleaning up and was feeding her when Kate came in from work. She no sooner walked in the door and put her things down when she blasted me with everything that was wrong with me. It was as though I couldn't do anything right, and it felt like she hated me!"

Teresa's son Adam and Kate have been married for four years and have been parents for almost two of those years. From the beginning, Teresa felt that she and Kate were close. Even before Adam and Kate married, Teresa and Kate talked openly with one another, and they made a point of spending time together whenever possible. Teresa had felt lucky to have the kind of relationship she had with her DIL since she knew many MILs have such a tense or tentative relationship at best. Teresa felt Kate was truly like a member of her family—a true daughter to her.

Kate has also enjoyed Teresa—at least most of the time. She has learned a lot from her over the years, but Kate is also a bit intimidated by her MIL. It's not that Teresa is mean or bossy, but she can be a strong, imposing figure to say the least, and Kate often finds herself deferring to Teresa because of this. Kate isn't happy with how this makes her feel— about herself, the situation, and at times about her MIL.

As much as Teresa and Kate enjoy each other, they each have their own way of parenting, keeping house, planning events, and so on. Because Teresa views Kate as one of her children now, she steps in whenever she can to make things easier for both Kate and Adam. She knows they have busy schedules and often seem to be at their wits' end trying to get things done around the house. Although Teresa struggles to understand how it is that her son and DIL operate this way, she tries not to say anything because she thinks that would only make things awkward and would probably hurt their feelings. She believes the best and most thoughtful thing to do would be to help them out whenever she can. And so when she goes to their house, she makes sure everything is picked up, the dishes are done, the clothes left in the dryer are folded—basically, she goes ahead and does whatever she feels needs to be done.

Kate has known her MIL doesn't really approve of the way she keeps house or her more casual style of doing things. Knowing this makes Kate feel bad about herself at times. She knows Teresa likes everything neat and in its place, which is fine, but Kate also knows that isn't her. It's too difficult for her to maintain that lifestyle and, to be honest, she doesn't see what the big deal is anyway. Her house is "lived in." And her husband doesn't seem to mind. At least Adam doesn't complain about it—most of the time.

Kate tries hard not to let her MIL's "helpfulness" get to her, but there are times when she just can't help getting annoyed. Kate's doubting herself is bad enough on its own, but when Teresa takes over, Kate's insecurity feels worse. It seems to Kate as though Teresa is judging her every time her MIL picks up the house or cleans up after them. It makes Kate feel like a child. And to Kate, there is nothing worse than that! Kate has made a point not to say anything to her MIL because she doesn't want to make waves, but she's afraid it may show in her behavior or on her face when she gets close to that breaking point.

Kate had initially chosen not to say anything to her husband, thinking that maybe if she just held out a while, Teresa's actions would either stop or Kate would start to feel differently about them. Neither was the case. So she began venting to Adam when she felt things building, which seemed to help at first.

Not long ago, Kate found herself struggling once more with her feelings about her MIL's involvement in their home life. "Why does your mom have to be so involved?" she asked Adam. "Every time I turn around, she is doing something in our house—*our house*! Does she even *think* about what she is doing and how it might make me feel? I'm a new wife and a new mom, and she comes along doing whatever she does as if I should be doing it her way—or in her eyes, the *right* way. She just assumes what she is doing is okay with me, or what I want her to do. She doesn't even *ask*, she just *does*!"

Not quite understanding why Kate was so upset with his mother helping, but not wanting to say anything to make her feel worse, Adam let Kate vent. When she was done, he gave her a hug and said, "I'm sorry Mom frustrates you so much. I think you're doing a great job juggling the baby, the house, your job, and me."

When Kate and Adam had their baby girl, they decided that they wanted both of their mothers to watch her at least one day a week. They felt this would give each of them some alone time with their granddaughter, as well as help the two of them. Both grandmothers were delighted with the prospect and had quickly fallen into a pleasant, rhythmic routine.

The next day was Teresa's day to watch the baby and Kate knew she'd be over any minute. Adam had already left for work, and Kate was running late. Although she tried to get things picked up, she barely had time to get the baby fed and herself dressed. Kate was almost ready when Teresa walked in, energetic as usual, looking like she was ready to take on the day full force. Just as Kate was walking out the door she remembered some vital instructions she needed to give Teresa about the baby, and she also needed to tell her about a repairman who was coming later in the day. After hurriedly letting Teresa know, she rushed out the door so she wouldn't be late for work.

Later that morning, Teresa took the baby to the park and while they were out, she bought some fresh flowers. *Kate will love these!* she thought, picking out a bouquet of colorful wildflowers. *I'm sure she doesn't always think to buy herself something like flowers.* When she and the baby got back to the house, Teresa arranged the blooms in a vase and placed them on the dining room table.

She'd just finished cleaning up when she realized Kate and Adam would soon be home. She decided she would go ahead and feed the baby to give Kate and Adam a chance to eat without having to tend to the baby first. A few minutes later, Kate walked in the door and was surprised by what she saw—*her baby being fed* and *flowers on the table!* Everything looked perfect. Kate could not describe how this made her feel—lesser-than, incompetent, maybe even impotent. Whatever she was feeling, it did not feel good.

"Why are you feeding the baby?" she asked her MIL accusingly. "I didn't ask you to do that."

Teresa was stunned. "I just thought I'd give you both a break so that you could eat in peace," she said, genuinely confused.

"Well, I don't need you deciding what we need a break from and what we don't," Kate stated as firmly as she could. She was not in the mood to deal with "Miss Perfect" right now, and she definitely couldn't take one more "perfect" moment of hers. "We do things differently around here and if you can't respect that, then maybe you don't need to be coming around. I don't tell you how to do things in your house, so what gives you the right to tell me how to do things here?"

Kate was on a roll. She couldn't seem to stop, and Teresa was on the verge of tears. She didn't understand where this was coming from. "I was just trying to help," she said. "Since when have I told you what to do in your house? In fact, I make a point of saying nothing about how you do things—*nothing*!" Teresa's voice escalated as she fought back her tears. "I've only tried to be helpful to you both."

"This is not helpful. It is hurtful!" Kate said, her angry eyes boring holes into her MIL. "If I want your help I'll ask for it, but I haven't. So please...*please* just stop doing everything. This isn't your home!"

"I'm sorry, Kate. I didn't mean to upset you, and I definitely did not intend to do anything that might hurt your feelings, *really*," Teresa said, wanting to make things right with her DIL, but still filled with so much confusion that she feared her words did not have enough conviction behind them to sound genuine. "If you don't want me helping you around the house, I won't. I just thought I could take some of the load off you. That's all." Even though Teresa was saying these things, she really wasn't sure why she needed to say them. Wasn't it obvious what she'd been trying to do? She really didn't understand what she had done that was so terribly wrong.

Kate wasn't sure what she had just done. Although she felt she was right to say what she said, she rarely showed those kinds of feelings to Teresa, and now she felt awkward about her outburst. She knew she had been holding this in for a long time, and while she wasn't sure why the words came out at that moment, she knew she couldn't take them back. It was how she felt, after all. Right now, all she wanted—*needed*—was for this situation with Teresa to be over. She didn't know where to go with it at this point. But she didn't have to wait long before relief came, because Teresa got up and said she was leaving.

CHAPTER 3

# The Blame Game

*Blaming your MIL or DIL is easy. Doing something
to change your relationship — to make it
better — takes courage.*

IF YOU CONNECT in any way to even one of the stories in the first
two chapters, you've probably felt at one time or another that your
situation was hopeless. You've done everything you can think of to
make things better, and yet nothing changes. Your in-law still treats
you badly. She still ignores your wishes. You still find yourself getting
anxious at the thought of being around her, knowing you'll be on guard,
thinking, *What will she do next?* or *What am I doing (or not doing)
that will upset her?*

This helpless feeling lingers, hanging in the air between the two of
you. Everything about this relationship feels impossible. This is when
you give up, accept the status quo, and tell yourself: *This is just the way
it's going to be.* It's not what you want, but you've resigned yourself to
the fact that your in-law is *never* going to change. After all, you've tried
everything you can think of, but your *in-law* is the problem. And not only
is the relationship not getting better, but sometimes you think it might
even be getting worse! So you do nothing.

If you don't quite feel this dire about your uncomfortable relationship with your in-law, maybe you just tell yourself the problems between you aren't all that bad. So why bother working on it? You don't really know what to do, or maybe it just seems easier to avoid the situation. After all, who likes confrontation or making a big deal out of things, right? If you're a DIL, you may decide that having no contact with your MIL is the best option—sidestepping the whole matter completely.

However, not dealing with these problems only makes them worse. At some point, the way you feel—anxious, nervous, angry, frustrated—will come out in your actions. This may be subtle or not so subtle, but either way, it will only create bigger problems because your in-law will react to those subtle or not-so-subtle actions of yours. This creates a snowball effect of negative actions and reactions.

Believe me, I know what this is like. I experienced it myself and allowed it to go on longer than I care to admit. However, feeling the relationship is hopeless does not mean that it really *is* hopeless. It just *feels* that way. One of the themes throughout my first MIL/DIL book, *Reluctantly Related: Secrets to Getting Along with Your Mother-in-Law or Daughter-in-Law*, is that one person *can* make a difference—*without* having to challenge or confront the other person.

The key is realizing that you do indeed have the power to make a difference. I know, this sounds abstract. And it may sound like some psychological jargon you've heard a thousand times before. But it happens to be true, and it's not quite as abstract as you may think. This concept is actually based in science, observed time and time again by experts in both family systems and group dynamics. And this is what it means: When one person in a relationship changes her behavior, the other person in the relationship has no choice but to also change *her* behavior.

If you're wondering why this is so, think about it for a minute. When you start behaving in a different way with someone, it's really not possible for that person to react in the same predictable way they always have because their actions will no longer fit the situation. It will no longer make sense for them to act in that same old way.

Here's an example:

Leanne's MIL seemed to always make some off-the-wall comment about Leanne at family gatherings, leaving Leanne feeling foolish, embarrassed, and self-conscious around the other family members. Not knowing how to handle these situations, Leanne would usually get red in the face and indicate through her body language that she felt awkward and uncomfortable. On those few occasions when Leanne would say something to her MIL about how her words made her feel, her MIL would shoot back, "I'm just joking. Don't be so sensitive!" This made Leanne feel even more defeated and hopeless about the situation ever changing, which in turn seemed to stoke the fire of her MIL continuing to feel she had power over Leanne.

When Leanne started using humor on her MIL during family gatherings, things started to change. Although Leanne still felt foolish, embarrassed, and a bit self-conscious in the beginning, she stuck with her new behavior: After her MIL would say something insensitive, Leanne would start to laugh or chuckle, shake her head, and agree with her MIL. At other times, she would take what her MIL said to an extreme, which then put the comment into perspective as being ridiculous. Her MIL appeared startled and taken aback, not really knowing how to respond. Leanne's action stopped her in her tracks. As time went on, her MIL quit making malicious comments toward Leanne, allowing Leanne to actually enjoy those family gatherings that had once been a nightmare for her.

Leanne's MIL started out needing to show Leanne that even though Leanne had married her son, the MIL still had all the power and importance in the family—particularly power over Leanne. But when Leanne changed how she responded to her MIL's behavior, she was able to shift the power balance away from her MIL and toward herself. Her MIL could no longer fall back on her line of "You're too sensitive" because Leanne did not confront or challenge her. In fact, she emphasized her MIL's words instead of shying away from them. This shift in Leanne's behavior put her MIL in a position to behave differently.

## When You Feel You "Hate" Your In-Law

When you don't deal with the issues between you and your in-law, the situation can often go too far. Here's an example from both the DIL's and the MIL's perspective.

### First, from the DIL's perspective:

Let's say your MIL said or did something that upset you. Instead of saying something to her about it, you decide it's best to say nothing. And then she does *something else*. Even though you feel your irritation building, you again decide to say nothing. And maybe a bit down the road she does or says *something else* that bothers you, but just as before, you say nothing to her. Your rationale goes something like this: *It's not worth saying anything. I don't even know what I would say that could actually make a difference. After all, she's so hard to talk to about anything!*

However, now you start to cringe at the thought of being around your MIL. The things she did and the feelings she stirred up inside you resurface at the mere thought of her—and even more so when you have to be around her. You feel the tension inside rise, your anger builds, and your body becomes rigid when she tries to talk to you or hug you. Now you find yourself coming up with reasons not to be around her.

### Now, from the MIL's perspective:

You are interacting with your DIL, completely unaware she is upset with you. You interact with her again. And again, you have no idea your DIL is having a problem with you. And before long, you notice your DIL has cooled toward you. You aren't sure why, but you say nothing because you are afraid to say anything for fear of your DIL's reaction.

As time goes by it seems to you that your DIL is avoiding you. You are not sure what to do. You've tried to feel her out to find out what is wrong, but everything with your DIL feels awkward and forced now. You feel the apprehension build. You feel like you are walking on eggshells whenever you are around her. You find yourself pulling back, yet you're also angry with your DIL for putting you in this position. The resentment mounts. You start rationalizing, thinking, *It's not worth it to fight this hard to see my son and grandkids. My DIL makes it impossible! And I don't want to make things more difficult for my son.*

Each negative situation or negative exchange builds on the next until either one or both of you feel as though you hate the other. Now, I know "hate" is a strong word, but it is a word that some MILs and DILs use to describe how they feel about each other. Interestingly, the experience of feeling "hate" is different for MILs than it is for DILs. It takes on a different purpose and stems from different underlying issues.

### MILs Who Feel They Hate Their DILs

When you feel hatred toward your DIL, you've now attached this word to her. Whenever you see her or think of her, this feeling of hate will bubble to the surface and end up establishing a life of its own—daughter-in-law/hate—all meld together. You will not be able to see your DIL without also feeling hate.

What you may not be aware of is that angry feelings like hate are typically secondary emotions. This means that they cover up other, more vulnerable feelings that you are afraid to share—even with yourself. You may feel hurt, devastated, wounded, overwhelmed, or a hundred other feelings about something your DIL said or did. But truly allowing yourself to feel the depth of these feelings (let alone showing others that you feel them) is too scary, so you protect yourself with feelings of anger, frustration, and yes, even hate. This happens without you even recognizing it. And herein lies the problem.

Let me break the process down so we can take a closer look:

- You feel hate toward your DIL, which creates a barrier—a dead end. You have no place to go when you feel hate.

- You've now attached this dead-end feeling to your DIL.

- But hate is not really the true feeling you are experiencing— it is a secondary emotion that protects you from what you actually feel.

- So here you are, aching to have a relationship with your DIL, but instead, you've created this "hate" barrier between you. This prevents you from figuring out a way to get close, even though this is exactly what you really want—to be close and have a real relationship with her.

Here's an example:

Mary is done! She is tired of the way Susan (her DIL) treats her, and she has decided it is time to just write her off—even if that means not seeing her son or grandchildren. She doesn't say she "hates" Susan, but her actions say it—her conscious, deliberate decision to remove herself indicates her feelings loud and clear.

Eventually Mary contacts me because her feelings toward her DIL were starting to affect her other relationships. As she shares her story, I begin to challenge her strong negative feelings toward Susan. Mary admits she hates Susan for how she treats her and because Susan's actions are preventing her from seeing her son and grandchildren.

We begin delving into her intense negative feelings toward Susan. Upon reflection, Mary begins to see that underneath her feelings of hatred are feelings of hurt, fear, and hopelessness. She realizes she is so afraid of having these feelings because, to her, that would mean more pain than she feels she can bear. These feelings make her feel powerless—whereas the feeling of hatred gives her a sense of power and control.

Instead of hating your DIL as a way to protect or deflect how vulnerable you feel, it is much better to actually get in touch with whatever you are really feeling underneath the hatred. Let yourself know and experience what those feelings really are and how they affect you. In doing this, you will be in a better position to deal with those scary, vulnerable feelings. Please note: I am *not* suggesting that you share these vulnerable feelings with your DIL. I *am* suggesting that you get in touch with them for yourself.

Once you are in touch with them, understand them, and accept them, you are able to move away from the hate feelings. You might be annoyed or frustrated with your DIL, but you will no longer be letting the "hate barrier" get in the way of having a relationship with her. This in turn will move you closer to creating what you truly want in your relationship with her.

So, how do you get in touch with what is underneath those feelings of hatred? Here are some steps to get you started:

1.  Think about your feeling of hatred toward your DIL.

2.  Write down her behavior and the situation that fostered this feeling, describing them in detail. Consider answering these questions:

    a.  What led up to the incident?

    b.  What did your DIL do or say?

    c.  *How* did she say or do it? In other words, what tone of voice or body language did she use?

    d.  What feelings were you actually feeling during and after she said or did whatever upset you?

3.  Now write down what vulnerable feelings are underneath the feeling of hate—in other words, what is the hate protecting you from feeling? Ask yourself:

    a.  What does it feel like to actually feel the vulnerable feelings?

    b.  What scares you about these feelings?

    c.  What would it mean or say about you if you were to allow yourself to experience these feelings?

    d.  Why is feeling vulnerable a bad thing?

## DILs Who Feel They Hate Their MILs

Feeling this strongly toward your MIL makes you want to have as little to do with her as possible. You want to avoid her altogether. But feeling this strongly about anyone, including your MIL, actually means this person matters to you. Otherwise, there'd be no reason to have such strong feelings.

Think about it this way: If a stranger, an acquaintance, or a casual friend did or said the same things your MIL did or said, you probably wouldn't hate that person. You might be frustrated. You might be annoyed. You might even be angry. But you probably wouldn't hate the other person because the emotional connection or investment you have in them is not as deep or as important to you. I realize this may not be what you want to hear, and it may also not be something you want to believe. But then ask yourself: Why do you feel this strongly about someone who doesn't matter?

So what is this feeling of hatred *really* about? Why are you feeling this much intensity? If you look at *why* she has this kind of impact on you, you will be able to understand yourself better, and you will be able to lessen the negative impact this feeling is having on *you*—which, in turn, will affect how you react or respond to the people around you.

To help you figure out what is going on, ask yourself:

- Do you feel as though you are not in control when you are around your MIL?

- Do you dislike how you feel about yourself when your MIL says or does these things that make you feel so strongly?

- Do you get upset with the way you react to what she says or does?

- Do your MIL's actions create a feeling of inadequacy or self-doubt within you?

- Do you feel devalued by what she says or does?

- Do you feel your MIL looms over you?

As you can see, this exercise is about you getting in touch with how your MIL's actions impact *you*. You respond to her actions based on the feelings she stirs up for you. As much as you may hate your MIL, that hatred feeling keeps you stuck in a place that hurts you, your husband, and your marriage. You may be investing so much energy into hating this woman that it is affecting every aspect of your life.

Here's Samantha's story:

Samantha is at her wits' end. She has tried everything she can think of to get her MIL to show her respect. Nothing Samantha does seems to make a difference. She has reached a point of no return. She can't stand to even hear her MIL's name, let alone spend time with her. Although somewhat sympathetic to what she is going through, Samantha's husband doesn't understand why his mother's actions cause such a reaction in his wife. The situation is now starting to affect their marriage.

When Samantha and her husband come to see me about the fights they have been having involving his mother, I listen to Samantha's feelings about her MIL and why she hates her so much. As Samantha shares her experiences and the emotions these experiences stir up, she begins to reflect on her feelings. She starts to see that her MIL's behavior and attitude toward her has caused feelings of doubt and uncertainty Samantha has about her judgments and decisions to surface—and even more importantly, Samantha recognizes that her MIL's behavior diminishes how she feels about herself.

Even if you think your situation isn't quite that bad, remember that your children are watching how you react to "loved" ones. They watch how you treat people you are supposed to care about—which means that you are their role model for how to treat family when *they* are older.

If you recognize yourself in this equation, take heart. It is indeed possible to put your feelings and your MIL into their respective places so that they do not clash, moving you out of that place of hate. Ask yourself the following questions:

- Do you *really* believe your MIL deliberately wants to hurt you?

- Do you *really* believe she wants to make you feel bad about yourself as a mother, as a wife, and as a person?

- Is she *really* that mean, malicious, and sadistic that she sought you out just so that she could watch you wince in pain?


Or could it be that your MIL:

- Didn't realize how her words may have sounded or how you might have interpreted her actions?

- Didn't really think before she spoke or acted?

- Is a self-centered person who may be overly anxious and says or does these kinds of things with *everyone*, not just you?

Then ask yourself:

- Does feeling hatred toward your MIL give you power?

- Does hanging on to this feeling give you a reason to push your MIL away, when what you *really* want is to have a good relationship with her?


Understanding what is behind this feeling of hatred allows you to put your feelings of hatred in perspective. It allows you to shift this feeling in a way that helps you create some emotional distance between your MIL's actions and your response. It allows you to deal with your issues and not take on what are hers.

Whether you are a MIL or DIL, moving beyond this pain can feel impossible, but it really isn't.

## Action Steps

- Identify why up to this point you have felt either hopeless or helpless to change your relationship with your in-law or why you've simply avoided making changes. (Your answer may be one or more of the reasons discussed already, or it may be a completely different reason.)

- Go through the steps outlined above for MILs who feel they hate their DILs or for DILs who feel they hate their MILs so you can get in touch with what you are really feeling.

- Write down five things you will do to begin changing your relationship with your in-law. Feel free to start out with small steps. Remember, each baby step moves you closer to where you want to be.

# CHAPTER 4

# Ignorance Isn't Bliss

*It is easier to avoid what we don't understand...*
*But the rewards are life changing when we take the*
*time to learn about what we don't know.*

THE MIL/DIL RELATIONSHIP is the most difficult and most tension-filled relationship in the family system—and it's also the most critical relationship in that system. In my first book, *Reluctantly Related: Secrets to Getting Along with Your Mother-in-Law or Daughter-in-Law,* I devoted a whole chapter to why this relationship between MILs and DILs is so difficult. Since writing that book, I've found there's even more to this story.

First, let me give you a quick overview from *Reluctantly Related* of the five factors that affect the MIL/DIL relationship and how these factors seriously contribute to its difficulties:

- **It's an artificial relationship:** Two women who did not choose to be in each other's lives are thrown together for one reason—the MIL's son and the DIL's husband.

- **Different stages and different emotional places:** The MIL has already been where the DIL is now and where the DIL is going. One is looking backward—one is looking forward.

- **Personal history and emotional baggage:** Our life experiences and our personal issues, which are formed because of the different challenges and situations we've faced in our lives, color our understanding and perceptions of interactions, situations, and events.

- **Perception:** The way we perceive and interpret behaviors, interactions, situations, and so on is filtered through our different life experiences and personal issues.

- **Reaction:** Our reactions to these different experiences are directly related to how we have perceived a particular situation or behavior.

The MIL/DIL relationship is extremely fragile. One wrong look, one inconsiderate word or behavior, or one off-putting remark can change this relationship forever. These five factors help to explain why this is the case. What has become even clearer, though, is that the MIL and DIL perpetually struggle to find the delicate balance that's needed in order for this relationship to feel comfortable and easy. It seems other family relationships, even other in-law relationships, can weather the storm much better than the MIL/DIL relationship.

The overall reason for the difficulty between the MIL and DIL is that there's an undercurrent of competition between them. You may be thinking, *I knew that! That is no big surprise.* But hold on—this competition may not be what you think it is. Most people assume this competition is for the husband's or the son's love, but that's not the case. The competition is for the *influence* that these two women have over him.

This is an unspoken—and often unidentified—competition. Most women feel something going on, but they're uncertain exactly what it is. They try to label it with the actions displayed by the other. For example, a DIL may be thinking, *His mother won't let go;* while a MIL might be thinking, *His wife wants to keep him from his family.* Labeling the situation in this way is really how each woman tries to make sense of and deal with this covert competition. So in other words, these statements or reactions are the *consequences* of this undercurrent of competition. They're not the actual issue.

Think about it for a minute. Your in-law says or does something. You feel frustrated, hurt, or possibly even angry, but more is going on with you than this one feeling. There's another component to what you're feeling—anxiety—that gets things rolling. Reacting to the anxiety is what contributes to the competition for influence.

Whether you're the MIL or the DIL, you typically react by labeling the other's behavior using statements like those mentioned earlier: "His mother won't let go," or "His wife wants to keep him from his family." You push back to get rid of the anxiety you are feeling. Your behavior, or should I say your *reaction*—as well as your in-law's reaction—is all about this undercurrent and misunderstood threat: losing the influence you have over your husband or son. And it's not just about losing this influence, it's about losing it to your in-law! And all of this occurs in a split second!

I think DILs may be more aware of this competitive component than MILs, but they often mislabel it and fail to see their role in it. They see it more as a MIL issue. What they don't recognize is that they *do* play a role in the competition, not to mention what that role is.

MILs, on the other hand, struggle to see this competition even when it is pointed out to them. A MIL will typically say, "But I let go of my son long ago. I know his wife is his priority, but...." It is this "but" that indicates the MIL is still struggling with her role or with her loss of influence in her son's life. Yes, she has let go on one level, but letting go occurs on *many* levels. (I will get into this more in a later chapter.)

As I mentioned previously, the MIL/DIL relationship is the most critical relationship within the family. Women are generally the key figures in any relationship, but when you look at an entire family system, including all the different in-laws—sisters-in-law, brothers-in-law, fathers-in-law, mothers-in-law, and daughters-in-law—as a whole, the MIL/DIL relationship has cornered the market on importance.

When a MIL and DIL do not get along, the conflict affects everyone in the family. People often feel the need to take sides, either openly or in a quieter, subtler way. Regardless, no one is immune from what is going on in this relationship.

Whatever the issues may be between the MIL and DIL, everyone in the family knows about them. They may not know the specifics, but they feel the tension, see the behaviors, and experience the stress. Unfortunately, each member of the family comes into the situation from their own perspective—meaning their own personal history and emotional baggage. As a result, it's difficult for any one of them to remain neutral. These other in-law relationships become colored by what the MIL and DIL do and say, which then keeps the whole "family pot" stirred.

## Family Dynamics of the MIL/DIL Conflict

Here are all the different things that are going on when MILs and DILs do not get along:

- The father-in-law (the MIL's husband) sees his wife hurting and in pain.

- The sister-in-law (the MIL's daughter) more than likely takes on the role of her mother's confidant in her struggle with the DIL. This may not only affect the daughter's relationship with her sister-in-law, but it may also affect her relationship with her brother.

- The other daughters-in-law/sisters-in-law (the MIL's other sons' wives) also become confidants for each other. After all, when one DIL doesn't get along with her MIL, she typically commiserates with the other DILs. It is often a common bond they have with one another.

- The brother(s)-in-law—the MIL's other son(s)—may try to stay out of the mess between his sister-in-law and his mother. But if this tension spills over onto his wife (in other words, if his sister-in-law gets angry with his wife if she does not agree with the issues she has with the MIL), he will want to shield his wife from any pain or hurt. He may also get upset with his brother if his brother's wife is causing too much havoc in the family.

- The husband/son is impacted because it's his mother and his wife who are feuding, which puts him right in the middle of what is going on between them.

- Children/grandchildren feel torn because they love their mom *and* they love their grandmother. (Remember, kids see grandparents very differently than the parents do. She is *their* grandma, after all.) Their relationship with her is typically nothing like the relationship the grandmother/MIL has with the DIL, or even like the relationship the grandmother/MIL has with her son. Children/grandchildren do not understand the issues that play out between adults; they notice only the behavior each of them displays, which can be confusing. They also learn from both their grandma and mom the way to treat people who matter to you.

- And then you have the DIL's side of the family. When they hear from their daughter or sister about how her in-laws treat her or behave around her, they will form their opinions of them based on what she tells them (as well as on their own personal history and emotional issues). They will then give her feedback, suggestions, and so on, based on that personal history combined with the DIL's one-sided perspective.

No one wants to believe—and typically no one *does* believe—that they are directly or indirectly hurting other people, particularly people they care about. Unfortunately, that is exactly what is occurring in this dynamic. As unintentional as it may be, both the MIL and DIL do end up hurting the other people in their family who love them.

Here's an example:

Jessica can't get over how her DIL is treating her. According to Jessica, her DIL's actions have made it clear that she doesn't have time to spend with her, nor will she allow Jessica's son and granddaughter to come over without her. And although Jessica tries to keep her feelings to herself, sometimes they spill over and she shares how she feels with her other son and her daughter.

Both of Jessica's other children really struggle when they see their mother so upset. To them this is just crazy. They know their mom isn't perfect, but she's not a monster! They think, *Why can't they all just get along?* In their own way they both try to console Jessica, resenting the position their sister-in-law has put their whole family in.

Now, what do you think happens when Jessica and all of her children/in-laws get together? How do you think Jessica's other children view their sister-in-law? How will they treat her?

Here is another example:

Tonya is tired of the way her MIL treats her. She feels as though her MIL has no respect for her, especially when it comes to her parenting. No matter what she says or how she says it, her in-laws ignore her and do whatever they want to do.

Tonya and her husband talk about his parents, particularly his mother, in an attempt to figure out how to handle them, but that isn't enough. Tonya still feels what she feels. And so she tells her mother what has been going on, hoping maybe her mother will have some ideas, or if nothing else, at least she will be someone who will understand how Tonya feels.

Her mother listens. She can tell how much Tonya is hurting and is angry that the in-laws are causing her daughter so much pain. She knows her daughter is a good person and a good mother. *These people have no right to treat my daughter this way!* she thinks. She gives Tonya some suggestions about how she can handle her in-laws, not realizing that much of what she is suggesting is clouded by the anger she is feeling.

What happens if Tonya takes her mother's advice, based on the fact that this advice is clouded by both her mother's anger and her need to protect her child? What happens if Tonya wants to work on having a better relationship with her MIL? Will her mother be able to be okay with that, since she is left with this horrific image of the in-laws? And if her mother isn't okay with it, how could that affect Tonya? How could it affect the in-laws?

As you can see, the MIL/DIL relationship is a powerful and long-reaching one. It does not just affect the MIL or the DIL. It affects *all* the other people in the family. Whether you feel it is your MIL or your DIL who is *really* causing the problem, each one has the ability to step up and stop the insanity. It is just a matter of making the decision to take the first step. After all, should it really matter *who is at fault* when you have so much to lose? Or is what matters most *who is willing to step up and make things better*?

## Bonds vs. Relationships

Relationships are extremely complex because there's more to them than what you see on the surface. Sometimes people have both a bond *and* a relationship with another person; sometimes they have a bond, but no real relationship; other times they have only a relationship, and no bond. Confusing, right? And what does all this mean anyway?

Although the difference between having a bond with someone and having a relationship with them can be baffling, not fully understanding this concept can cause havoc in a MIL/DIL relationship. For example, a MIL assumes that the close bond (and possibly close relationship) she had with her son should translate into their having a similarly close relationship well into his adult years. Yet MILs often confuse the close bond they have with their son with having a close relationship with him. And this is where the struggle begins. A MIL will typically measure the current closeness she now has with her son by assessing how often she talks with him, how much actual time she spends with him, the depth of personal information he shares with her, and so on. She is confusing the *bond* she has with her son (and possibly the relationship she had with him when he was growing up) with the *relationship* she has with him now as an adult.

The DIL, on the other hand, often senses the close bond her husband has with his mother, and she interprets this bond to be the same as their relationship. When doing this, she will think their "relationship" is too close. This then makes the DIL hyper-vigilant to any and all interaction between her husband and his mother, often misreading these interactions as more than they are. And so the struggle between the two women begins! The MIL feels the DIL is preventing her and her son from having their close relationship, and the DIL feels she is protecting her husband (and her relationship with him) from having three people in their marriage instead of two.

When MILs and DILs understand the difference between a bond and a relationship, this cuts down on this struggle between them and enables them to see each other much more accurately. Let me explain a bit more about the difference between these two concepts.

## A Bond

Having a bond with someone is not the same as having a relationship. You can have a bond—a connection with another person at a deep level—for many different reasons, including the nature of your relationship with them. For example, a parent and child often have a bond. Two people can have a bond with one another because they share a mutual or similar circumstance, as is frequently found among survivors of any kind. A bond does not have agendas or expectations. It doesn't matter how often you see each other or even *if* you see each other; it doesn't matter what type of relationship—or lack of relationship—you may have with one another. The bond is something you both feel—you *know* it is there because you feel its presence. You may not be able to explain it in words, but as I said, you *know* it's there. It does not waver.

However, just because you have a bond with someone doesn't always mean you have an ongoing relationship with this person. I've had clients tell me, "I have a bond with my mother, but I don't really have a relationship with her." Or "I know I have this connection with my sister, but we don't really have anything else in common." Or "Although I rarely see my best friend from college anymore, when we do see each other, it's as though we can pick up where we left off. We just connect in a way I can't explain." These are all examples of bonds.

A bond is much deeper than any relationship can be because it transcends the various components that make up a relationship.

## A Relationship

A relationship, on the other hand, is more of a living entity. Unlike a bond, a relationship ebbs and flows. It will change, grow, or cease to exist depending on the people involved. To stay alive and thrive, it must be nurtured. One factor that plays into any type of relationship is that, unlike bonds, relationships have expectations. Usually these expectations are unspoken but nevertheless they are critical to making the relationship work and endure.

As we all know through our life experiences, if we don't work at a relationship it will not last—that is one of the unspoken expectations. Working at it can mean many things depending on the type of relationship we have. A marital relationship has different expectations than a friendship, and a friendship has different expectations than a work relationship. But all relationships have at least one thing in common—you have to make an effort to maintain the relationship.

Relationships also vary in quality. You can have deep, committed relationships that last a lifetime. These types of relationships are built on commonalities, loyalty, communication, and most important, trust. These relationships have the highest expectations, but they're also the most rewarding.

Other relationships are more casual or even "relationships of convenience." Yes, commonality exists here as well, but your willingness to risk and be vulnerable is less likely, due to the nature of the relationship. That doesn't mean these relationships are not important, it just means they are different. In reality, we all have different kinds of relationships for different reasons. This is normal.

With most relationships, we make a choice whether or not to be in them, but obviously this isn't always true. When you are in a relationship you did not choose, as is the case with the MIL/DIL relationship, you must put in extra effort to make it work. You may have to really search to find that commonality or to find something about the other person that you like, and then you can grow into the relationship from there.

## Action Steps

*For MILs:*

- Identify how your relationship with your DIL is affecting the other members of your family.
- Name some constructive actions you can take to make things less tense and uncomfortable for the other family members.
- Describe the relationship you had with your son when he was growing up.
- Identify whether your relationship is a bond, a relationship, or both.
- If it's both, separate which part is a bond and which part is a relationship.
- Reflect on how can you maintain the bond with your son, while at the same time allow the relationship to change.

*For DILs:*

- Identify how your relationship with your MIL is affecting your relationships with the other members of your husband's family.
- Name some constructive actions you can take to make things less awkward and tense for your husband with regard to his family.
- Identify how your relationship with members of your husband's family affects your marriage.
- Describe the relationship your husband has with his mother.
- Identify what part of this is a bond and what part is a relationship.
- Reflect on how you can allow your husband's bond with his mother to remain intact, while their relationship changes.

# CHAPTER 5

# Clearing the Way

*Sometimes, without realizing it, we get in our own way of having the relationship we want. At those moments, we just need to step aside.*

NOW THAT YOU HAVE a better understanding of the overall struggle found in the MIL/DIL relationship and you have some clarity about the difference between a bond and a relationship, you're ready to get to work. You're now in a position to create some changes within *you* that will begin a change in your relationship with your MIL or DIL.

However, I first want to warn you about a few things that have the potential to sabotage you along the way. It's important to be ready for them because any kind of derailment, no matter how minor, can knock you off track permanently if you are not careful. But knowledge is power, right? So here is a chance to catch yourself *before* you are in the situation.

## Heightened Emotions

When you and your in-law are in a situation that gets you (or her) riled up, the emotions on either or both sides often cause you to draw lines, raise barriers, and have words with each other. She said or did something that hurt you. You feel victimized by her. What she said was wrong! How she perceived you or your actions was wrong! And this is where you get stuck. Your initial inclination is to set the record straight—to get her to see things more accurately. Unfortunately, the more you try, the worse things get between the two of you. She digs her heels in with each rationale or defensive word you say, until it escalates to the point of no return—and you fall into that black hole, that abyss that you so fear and dread.

Here's an example:

You are talking to your in-law and you notice that things are getting tense. You are not sure if she's upset with you, if she's about to confront you, or what—but you feel yourself getting anxious and a bit defensive, even though you haven't said anything yet. You then try to "fix" it, but you notice the conversation isn't going well. You are not sure what is going on, but you *do* know it doesn't feel good. Your anxiety climbs higher. You notice your body tensing up. Your breathing gets tighter and tighter and you get that unsettled feeling in the pit of your stomach. You feel your walls go up higher and higher. And now, as she is talking, your thoughts are racing as you plan in your head exactly what you want to say back to her.

What do you notice when you read this scenario? If you take a step back while you read it, you will see it: You are no longer listening. Once you begin to notice the changes in your body, the heightened emotions, and that inner dialogue of what you anticipate saying back to her, you are no longer able to listen to what she is saying. Your focus is on yourself, not on her. Your focus is now on how you are going to explain yourself, defend yourself, challenge her, or push her away. What you are not focused on is *listening.*

This is where you become stuck. And it's not just you who is stuck. She becomes stuck as well. You believe you are right. Your in-law thinks *she* is right. You think, *If I can just get her to see it from my perspective, she will understand. She will see I'm right.* However, from your in-law's perspective, if you are right, then she must be wrong—and therein lies the struggle. The more you try to reason with her, show her your side of things, the more she will dig her heels in and stay with her position.

I am aware that at that moment you are all revved up. You are upset with her and believe she is being unfair, maybe even ridiculous. However, expressing your feelings, trying to convince her that you did not do or say what she thinks you did or said won't get you want you want. As hard as it may be, this is the time to look at the bigger picture. What do you want in the long term: to be right or to have a relationship with your in-law (if for no other reason than for the sake of your husband or son, children or grandchildren)?

If you really want her to hear what *you* are saying, you have to be willing to listen to *her* first. You have to let her see that what she feels and what she thinks matters to you, regardless of whether she is right or wrong. It's about *listening* to her—not *agreeing* with her. It's about letting her see that she matters enough to you that you want to know what she is feeling, what she is thinking, and how she perceives the situation.

I realize this is not an easy task, but it is a necessary one if you want to create a better relationship with your MIL or DIL. If you think about yourself for a moment, you will realize that when you feel really emotional about something, and the other person involved listens to your feelings and really hears the emotional pain you are in, you begin to settle down. You soften because you  feel heard. You feel they get it. It's such a great feeling because, let's be honest, most of us do not feel anyone really listens or gets our emotional pain. And when someone does, it makes all the difference in the world.

Understanding your in-law's perspective is not just about helping her feel heard. This also creates an opportunity for you. Once you understand how she perceives the situation, you are in a better position to respond in a way that will get a more favorable response from her. When you truly listen, you create a shift in both of you—a shift that takes you from that negative, painful place where you started to a place that is more positive and more hopeful.

## Passive-Aggressive Behavior

Passive-aggressive behavior is the next thing to look out for. Here's how it manifests: Your MIL or DIL acts as though she is fine with whatever you do or say, yet later you find out she is upset, angry, or maybe even livid. She never says anything *directly* to you when she doesn't like what you've said or done, yet her *behavior* makes it perfectly clear she is incensed. She may always be late to an event you are hosting, refuse to talk to you (or give you short, terse, one-word answers), avoid you altogether, or maybe even display malicious subterfuge (such as those undermining "accidental" oversights). No matter what she says or doesn't say, her actions are speaking volumes. Believe me, this is not your imagination. This is called passive-aggressive behavior, and it is very real.

Dealing with passive-aggressive behavior (appearing to comply and behave appropriately on the surface, but actually behaving negatively and defiantly in a covert manner) can be incredibly difficult, draining, and frustrating. With this type of behavior, anger is not expressed openly, instead emerging in subtle ways in an attempt to avoid any form of confrontation. You can see what is going on when it is directed at you, but if you point it out to her, she looks at you as if you are crazy, denying what you know to be true but cannot prove.

MILs and DILs whose in-laws behave passive aggressively often say to me, "Why doesn't she just tell me if she doesn't like something? I can deal with that! Instead, she does this 'everything is fine, but it really isn't' kind of thing that makes it impossible to trust her and have a real relationship with her."

It helps to keep in mind that people aren't passive aggressive because they think being this way is a wonderful way to be. They behave this way because this is how they have learned to cope with uncomfortable situations, particularly with people who matter to them. It is common for someone who feels inadequate and/or disempowered *and* who is upset with, disagrees with, or doesn't like what another person says or does to express themselves through passive-aggressive behavior.

The passive-aggressive person typically feels inferior or afraid of the person they are upset with. They fear disapproval, abandonment, or worse. On top of this, they have never been shown or taught how to deal with uncomfortable feelings or situations. Due to this fear and sense of inadequacy, expressing their disagreement or dislike indirectly (in a passive way) feels safer to them than expressing these feelings openly and directly. This is how they have learned to cope with these difficult situations.

I know this may not sound rational, but coping strategies are not necessarily rational. They are often strategies that worked well when someone was a child, but these same coping strategies work less effectively when the person reaches adulthood. Unfortunately, we tend to use the coping strategies we know—until we learn better ones.

MILs and DILs express their passive-aggressive behavior in different ways. Much of this has to do with their roles in the relationship. A MIL has less power than a DIL because to her, the DIL holds all the cards—her son and grandchildren. However, a DIL can feel ineffectual, which leads her to sometimes use drastic measures to make her point.

For example, a MIL may play the martyr, completely ignoring what her DIL has said about rules or expectations, or she may show up late to an event her DIL is having. A DIL, on the other hand, may avoid her MIL (by staying in another room when the MIL comes to visit or by making sure she is not home when the MIL comes to her house), "forget" to include the MIL for special events (particularly those that involved the grandchildren), or criticize her MIL to a third party in an attempt to influence this person. Regardless of how one expresses this behavior, the goal is the same—to frustrate the other person and make them angry. It is as though she wants *you* to feel what *she* feels. However, this type of behavior is rarely, if ever, effective in getting her what she wants.

The husband/son can add fuel to the fire of a stressful MIL/DIL relationship by displaying passive-aggressive behavior as well. Typically in these situations, he allows things to happen, and he can even set it up to some degree, yet when you point it out to him, he acts as though he is helpless to change the situation.

Here is an example:

Sam's wife Catherine and his mother Debra have had a tense relationship for quite some time. Debra is devastated that she hasn't been allowed to see her son or grandchildren in almost a year. She missed both Thanksgiving and Christmas with them, and now her grandson's birthday is coming up. She has tried to make contact, but Catherine is ignoring her attempts. When Debra spoke with her son about it, all he said was, "I don't know what to say. I don't want to make things worse around here." This left Debra feeling even more helpless and really furious with her DIL for putting everyone in this situation.

Catherine, on the other hand, is frustrated at her MIL's lack of respect for her and her family. She has tried talking to her husband, but all he says to her is, "I don't know what to say to my mom. You know how she can be." Catherine is protective of her husband and hates to see him feeling this way. She is also tired of the drama his mother's visits seem to create and the toll it takes on the two of them. So she decided a while back to "handle" the situation with his mother herself. She refuses to have anything to do with Debra and encourages her husband to do the same. Although it may not be ideal, her husband seems okay with how she has chosen to handle the situation. Not only does he go along with it, but he also has not questioned it or suggested a better solution.

As you can see, this situation is bigger than the two perspectives described by the MIL and DIL. The key component in this situation is the husband/son. His passive-aggressive behavior set up an ugly situation between his wife and his mother. And the worst part of this is that both his wife and his mother see him as "poor Sam." His helplessness makes the atmosphere ripe for just this type of scenario. Worse yet, his wife is the one who ends up being blamed, and he is allowing this to happen.

Now that you have an understanding about passive-aggressive behavior in others, it is time to look and see if *you* are the one who may be passive aggressive. As I am sure you know, it's always easier to see behaviors you don't like in other people, but there comes a time when you need to be willing to look at yourself and see if maybe it is *your* behavior that is causing the problem (or at least part of the problem).

With this in mind, ask yourself the following questions. Do you:

- Habitually avoid your in-law when she comes to your house or do you regularly show up late to her events?

- Give your in-law the silent treatment or give terse one-word answers when she asks you questions or tries to engage with you?

- Criticize your in-law to other people in an attempt to sway them to your point of view?

- Use sarcasm, off-the-wall jokes, put-downs, and so on under the pretense of humor toward your in-law?

- Say you're fine, but then pout, play the martyr, covertly punish your in-law, or complain to your husband/son about your in-law's actions?

As I said earlier, passive-aggressive behavior is a coping strategy. It is something you learned—so that means it is something you can unlearn, too. When you are willing to look honestly at your own actions, you are demonstrating strength, courage, and maturity. You are saying, "I am human and I make mistakes. But I am willing to look at myself so that I can help my relationships flourish." In the end, this will make you a happier person.

### Blurring Boundaries

One of the most difficult challenges any of us face is making sure that we are seeing people for who they are as opposed to who we *think* they are. This plays a particularly important role in those relationships we have with people who matter to us or people who *should* matter to us. I say "should" because this gets to the crux of my point. Your in-law *should* matter to you for no other reason than your husband or son loves her. If you feel your in-law does not matter to you at all or you have strong negative feelings toward her, then this section is something you will want to pay close attention to.

What do I mean by blurring relationships? This occurs when we transfer the attitudes, feelings, and desires of those who were significant to us in our early childhood onto people in our current, adult life. In other words, different encounters or situations today can trigger familiar feelings related to previous encounters or situations from our childhood.

We all have this experience. We all blur relationships at one time or another. It could be that your co-worker reminds you of your aunt, who knew nothing about boundaries and was always overstepping them. Due to this history, the feelings you had about your aunt start to surface whenever you are around your co-worker, and you avoid that person just as you avoided (or tried your best to avoid) your aunt. Or maybe your neighbor presents herself just like your mother, as a victim—helpless and never responsible for what occurs in her life. And so you instantly feel infuriated every time you run into her, regardless of whether she says something to you or not.

In the case of a MIL and DIL, this blurring of relationships occurs when the MIL or DIL believes that her in-law is directing negative emotions—such as rejection, criticism, disapproval, or disappointment— toward her, even when this impression does not correspond with what the in-law is actually doing or saying. In other words, even though the in-law is neutral or even positive in her response, the MIL or DIL "reads" a negative intention from her.

Here are a few examples:

Erica is not sure what just happened, but she can tell her DIL is upset with her. All she did was mention to Beth that she would like to have her family together for dinner and then ask if they'd come over on Friday night. She didn't make a big deal about it—it was just a casual invitation. But that's not how Beth experienced it. This "invitation" sounded so familiar. It may have sounded like a casual question, but to Beth, the question was heavily laced with expectation. She found herself bristling at the thought of attending.

Kathy was excited that her son and DIL were coming to visit. She had been planning for a month. Her son and his wife Rachel had barely walked in the door when Kathy started offering them food that she had prepared just for them—including many things she knew they liked. They had been traveling all day. It was late, and both her son and Rachel were tired. Rachel nibbled on a few things, but she really just wanted to get some sleep. Finally, she let Kathy know she was going to bed. Kathy was devastated. She couldn't believe that Rachel was being so rude.

In both of these situations, relationships from the past are being blurred with the relationship of the present. The bristling feeling Beth felt when Erica invited them over for dinner was the same feeling Beth always got when her mother asked something of her yet really meant "You *will* do this." It stirred up feelings of powerlessness, weakness, and helplessness in Beth.

On the other hand, Kathy wanted to do something that would make her son and his wife happy, so they'd be glad that they were with her, just as she would try to do things to get her dad's love and approval when she was a young girl. When Rachel ate very little and, in Kathy's eyes, seemed disinterested in her efforts, this triggered the same feeling—devastation—that Kathy felt with her dad and his disinterest in her.

The problem with blurring relationships is that you are not connecting with the person in front of you, but instead relating to a template, which is often quite different from that person in the present moment. You are treating your MIL or DIL like your mother, father, grandmother, or whoever significantly impacted you years ago, when in reality she is nothing like them.

It's also important to keep in mind that this blurring of relationships is not something you are typically aware of at the time. You *think* this is how you feel based on what your MIL or DIL did or said. However, in actuality you are really reacting to an old feeling that was created years ago. When a potentially similar situation occurs, you unknowingly plug this "old feeling" (and all its intentions) into the current situation.

## Action Steps

- List how you prevent yourself from having the relationship you want with your MIL or DIL.

- Identify if your in-law, spouse, or you are displaying the coping strategy of passive-aggressive behavior.

- Pinpoint some areas where you are most vulnerable to blurring the relationship between your in-law and someone in your past.

# CHAPTER 6

# It's in the Details

*Negativity is a blinder that prevents us from*
*seeing anything positive that tries to shine through.*

WHEN MILS FIND OUT their sons are engaged and getting married, they often visualize what their relationship with their future DILs will be like, imagining the closeness they have had with their sons parlaying into closeness with their DILs. As MILs imagine these scenarios, they will replay them over and over in their heads.

DILs, on the other hand, typically don't think much about what it will be like to have a MIL. The focus of most DILs is on getting married—including the wedding and all the details that go into planning a wedding—and *being* married, building a relationship with their husbands, creating a home together, and so on. As you can see, with the MIL thinking and fantasying too much about what she hopes for this relationship and the DIL not thinking about it at all, they are already off to a challenging start.

And then something happens. Or maybe several things happen. You may be able to pinpoint exactly what occurred and when, or maybe you can't, but what you *do* know is that things between you and your in-law have gone awry. It has gotten to the point that either you are afraid to do anything at all around her for fear you will make the situation worse, or you'd rather just not have to deal with her at all.

When you get mired in the stress and strain of the MIL/DIL relationship, you often cannot get beyond the drama and misery. Everything you see, feel, and experience in this relationship is negative. The hurt and pain have gotten so big that every time you think about your MIL or DIL, let alone when you are physically around her, that's all you can think about. Everything she says and does seems to reinforce whatever you are already feeling, and there's no end in sight.

Then you finally reach a point where you know that if things are ever going to be better between you, you are going to have to do some things differently. And so you change some of your behavior in an attempt to elicit a change in your in-law. Nothing happens. You try again. Nothing happens. No matter what you do, her behavior never seems to change in the way you'd hoped—to a place where you can co-exist with her in a pleasant, comfortable way.

This sets up another challenge: When all you've seen from your in-law so far is negative behavior, it's incredibly difficult to notice anything positive. All you see is what *isn't* changing.

### Rebecca's Story

Rebecca's situation is a good example. During one session, I helped her identify several specific things she could do differently to start to change how her DIL behaved toward her. Her homework was to try some of them. The next time I saw her, we discussed the results. "I don't really have anything to report. Nothing is really different," she told me in a flat, discouraged tone. "Maybe I'm asking too much or expecting too much; I don't know. Amy is still being the same negative person she has always been around me."

I asked her to elaborate on the specific things she did differently during their last visit together and the specific reactions she got from her DIL. I asked her for as much detail about their interaction as possible so that I had a clear picture of what happened. And so Rebecca told me about Amy arriving late to the family gathering, not greeting her when she did come in, saying little to anyone during dinner, and so on.

Rebecca also mentioned that the whole family, including Amy, watched a movie together, but her DIL refused to sit next to her. Even though Rebecca had asked her if she wanted to sit on the couch, Amy chose to sit on the floor next to the couch. Rebecca also said that during the movie, she'd heard Amy talking to Rebecca's other DIL about a jacket Amy's daughter received as a birthday gift; Rebecca felt Amy's talking during the movie was a bit rude.

As she shared the details, it was clear to me that while her DIL's behavior was pretty much the same as it had always been, I also heard Rebecca mention some small yet encouraging behavior that showed a bit of a positive shift in Amy. For example:

1.  Although Amy came late to the family event, the fact that she came at all was a change, as she typically found an excuse not to come to anything on her husband's side of the family.

2.  The fact that Amy sat down with the family to watch a movie was different because usually she would go into another room or spend time with the kids to avoid interacting with her husband's family.

3.  Although Amy did not agree to sit next to Rebecca, she did sit close to her and remained there throughout the movie. She also turned down Rebecca's invitation to sit on the couch in an appropriate and even pleasant way.

4.  Talking with another DIL (albeit during the movie) was also something that Amy rarely did—and yet, here she was chatting with her.

5.  The jacket Amy was discussing was one that *Rebecca* had bought for her granddaughter. Not only did Amy say how much her daughter loved the jacket, but she also commented that *she* liked it as well.

Although I pointed out these small behavioral shifts to Rebecca, she was a bit reluctant to see them as positive steps toward change. "Well, I guess you're right," she said, "but Amy was still her same unpleasant self."

Rebecca's response is a common one. She has an idea of what she wants to see in her DIL's behavior, but when she doesn't see it right away, she gets discouraged and gives up. Herein lies the two-fold problem: 1) having a general idea of what you want to see as opposed to identifying some specific demonstrations of the general behavior you desire, and 2) expecting behaviors to go directly from all bad to all better.

## Abstract Thinking

Let me start by addressing the first part of this two-fold problem. One of biggest quandaries we all have is that we talk and think in abstract concepts as if they are concrete and tangible. For example, we will say, "I want her to be nice to me," "I wish she was more pleasant around me," or "I want her to be respectful of me." If we were to hear someone else make these statements, we would nod our heads, understanding the gist of what they were saying. However, these are still abstract concepts that make it difficult for us to recognize when someone is actually doing what we say we want them to do.

Let me explain further. When we are in a relationship that repeatedly feels lacking in some way, we tend to focus on that sense of lacking—what we aren't getting. It's hard to notice anything positive, and we tend to adapt an "all-or-nothing" mindset: Either we end up experiencing this abstract concept that we believe will make us feel good inside, or we end up with nothing. And this, then, sets us up to fail at getting what we want. Why? Our expectation is that we will realize this abstract concept when we experience this "good feeling." In other words, I will know when I get what I want when I go from feeling bad in some way to feeling good. But not only is this *not* the best measure of knowing you're getting what you want, but it also makes it too easy for you to hastily give up when you don't think you're getting what you desire.

The drawback to setting goals using abstract concepts is that these concepts really don't mean anything. They do not give you a clear picture of what you actually want. Think about it for a moment. What does "I want her to be nice to me" really *mean?* Saying, "I'll know it when it happens" (which is what we typically say to ourselves) isn't valid because we *don't* know it when we see it. In fact, like Rebecca, we often don't see it *at all!* We are too focused on everything we *aren't* getting to notice even the slightest movement toward getting something that we *do* want.

This is where clarity comes into play. For you to really distinguish the behavior you say you want, you first have to have a clear picture of what that behavior would look like. Otherwise, how will you know when you get it? Saying you want your in-law to be nice to you, for example, or to show you respect actually involves *many* different potential behaviors, not just one behavior. So you need to be able to detect *all* the different small behaviors that make up your abstract concept of "being nice," "showing respect," or whatever it is you want from your in-law.

Once you've determined all those small behaviors that make up the larger, more abstract concept, you will be able to visualize each of these small behaviors in your mind's eye, which in turn makes it easier for you to recognize them when you get them. Only by recognizing all these individual smaller behaviors will you be able to *know it when you see it.*

So if your goal is for your in-law to be nice to you, for example, some of the smaller concrete behaviors you could list might be her maintaining eye contact with you, smiling at you, having short dialogues with you, remaining in the same room as you, initiating contact with you, and so on. Making this list now makes it possible for you to look for these behaviors when you are around your in-law to help you gauge if and when your in-law is demonstrating "nice" behavior.

Now, keep in mind she may not always demonstrate every single one of these behaviors every single time you are together, but as you see her doing even one of these, you'll be less apt to lump all of her actions into statements like, "My in-law is just being her same old negative self." You are able to see her behavior more realistically, and you can see more of a balance between her negative and positive actions.

*Any* positive behavior you see her display is an opportunity for you to reinforce that behavior, which encourages her to keep showing it. (For example, if you see that she smiled at you, even if it was a brief smile, and you smile back at her, she's much more likely to smile at you again than she would be if you didn't really focus on the fact that she smiled and so didn't respond in kind.) This reinforcement creates a positive cycle—positive actions create more positive actions, instead of that vicious cycle of negative actions creating more negative actions.

## Realistic Timing

The second part of the two-fold problem—expecting behaviors to go instantly from all bad to all better—can also play into feelings of dejection and hopelessness. Again, we know what we want to see, but what we typically focus on is the result. *I acted differently,* we think, *so why didn't she respond the way I hoped?*

As great as it would be to have people change their behaviors overnight, behavioral change just doesn't work that way. Change occurs gradually, over time. After all, behavior patterns are just that—patterns that you repeat over and over, regularly and consistently. Once you've created a particular pattern of behaving, you don't think about it, you just respond using this behavior. Changing behavior, then, is a process that takes time and a desire on your part *to* change. It's that way with your in-law, as well. So you need to accept the fact that the bigger behavioral change you want will occur through small steps—again, steps that you can reinforce to encourage her to display them more often.

I should mention that your reinforcing her small behavioral changes also reinforces *your* ability to discern those small steps as your in-law moves closer to the behavior you are looking for from her. This in turn helps you see she is making progress toward change. You will become increasingly more aware of these subtle changes when she makes them, and your positive reinforcement of her changes will create a momentum for *both* of you to continue taking these small baby steps to a more positive place. In other words, each time you see a small positive step and your in-law feels your positive reinforcement, you both feel the desire to continue. This is how you go from all bad to all better (or at least much, much better)—by helping her move through *all* the steps in between those two extremes.

Let's go back to Rebecca's situation for a minute. Rebecca was so focused on what she ultimately wanted to see in her DIL's behavior (the all better) that she couldn't see any of the smaller steps Amy *did* make toward this change (the somewhat better). She completely missed or discounted the fact that her DIL showed up at all, that she sat and watched a movie with the family, that she was polite and appropriate when she responded to Rebecca's request to sit next to her, and so on. She was looking for her DIL to go from where she was—displaying only negative all-bad behavior—to displaying warm, fuzzy, accommodating all-better behavior. And because of this, she missed the smaller, yet important positive behaviors her DIL did display that were signs she was moving in the right direction.

I know this has been a lot of information to grasp, so here is a brief summary to help you review the main points and make sense of it all:

1. Your natural tendency is to focus on what your in-law is *not* doing, rather than to focus on anything positive she *is* doing— particularly when these positive behaviors are small and subtle.

2. In general, all of us think and speak in abstracts when we say how we want someone else to behave, which makes it difficult for us to recognize concrete behavioral changes.

3. It is important, then, to clarify this abstraction by being as specific as possible about what the desired behavior would actually look like.

4. Getting specific involves identifying all the many smaller, subtler behaviors that would indicate your in-law is moving closer to your more general desired goal.

5. The key is to watch for these baby steps, and when you see them, reinforce them by reacting in a positive, appreciative manner.

## Action Steps

- Write down what you want in general terms in your relationship with your MIL or DIL.

- Name one thing you would like to see different in your in-law's behavior. (This will be an abstract concept.)

- Taking that concept, break it down into specific behaviors that fit the concept, making a list of as many of these smaller, intermediate steps that you can think of. Get as concrete as you can so that you clarify for yourself what it is you want and so you are able to recognize your in-law's progress when she makes it.

- Watch for these smaller steps, and reinforce them when you see them.

# CHAPTER 7

# Independence Day

*The greatest gift we can give our children is independence.*
*Getting there is often easier for them than it is for us.*

BEING A PARENT IS COMPLICATED. No rulebooks exist to help us figure out what we are supposed to be doing when. As difficult as parenting is when children are young, we sometimes find it feels harder when they grow up. What is our role as a parent with a child who is now an adult? What does being a parent look like at this stage of the game?

What makes this so complicated is that being a parent isn't something you can just turn on and off. It's one of the ways you define yourself. It's who you are. But even though you will always be a parent, your role as a parent *does* (and needs to) change.

Mothers struggle with this more than fathers do. And whether you are the mother of a son or of a daughter, letting go of your child is necessary for them to grow into the adult he or she was meant to be. Janice's story is a good example. When she came to see me, she was angry and upset, but mostly heartbroken.

"My son and I have always been close," Janice shared, holding back her tears as best she could. "Even though he has been on his own for quite some time, he has always called once a week or once every two weeks. We didn't necessarily talk for a long time—the conversation was usually a quick update on what was going on in his life. Or if he needed to, he'd ask my opinion about something."

As I delved further into the situation, Janice was clear with me that she had emotionally separated from her son in a healthy way and that he was his own man. She was also quick to say that even before he married, he hadn't needed her in the same way he did when he was younger. To Janice, though, things changed drastically between her and her son once he married. He was no longer the son she knew. For the first time, he was truly distant and unwilling to share with her as he had done in the past.

"I don't know what happened," Janice lamented. "Since he's been married he hardly calls at all. When he finally does call, it's usually when he is in the car on his way home from work. So I find myself having to call him just to find out what is going on in his life. And when I do call he seems short, distracted, and almost angry with me. He was never like this before he got married. I think his wife is threatened by me for some reason. I think she doesn't like him talking to me, and so she gives him a hard time about it."

Janice's belief that she has emotionally let go of her son is only a partial truth. Yes, she *has* let go of him emotionally, but only on *one*

level. Emotionally separating and growing into the man a son needs to be is a process that occurs over time and in stages. For example, how a son sees his mother and her role in his life will be different when he's in his 20s than it will be when he is in his 30s, his 40s, and so on. This will (and should) happen regardless of whether he marries or not.

Another milestone that affects your son's sense of being a man is marriage. His pulling away is less about what his wife says or doesn't say, and more about how he sees himself and his view of "family" once he is married. He sees his family as "my wife and me." And when they have children, he sees his family as "my wife, my kids, and me." This is not a slight against you or his family of origin; it's more about his priorities and what being a man is all about for him. If you think about your own husband for a minute, you'll recognize something similar. He loves his mother, but his priorities are with you. He probably doesn't talk to his mom once a week, or ask for her opinions, or share intimate details about his life with her. Your son is no different. (It just *feels* different to you.)

## The Son's Part

Letting go on all the different levels is difficult because having less contact with your son, having him be less open, and having him be different from the boy you remember him as when he was living at home makes you feel less important in his life—less important to *him*. So before you automatically assume your son has pulled away because of his wife, consider some of these other possibilities:

1. He is moving through another level of his developmental transition from your *child* to the *man* he is supposed to be. He is not pulling away because he loves you less or wants you to feel excluded. As he matures and grows further into manhood, he feels the need and desire to share less with you. Men want and need to figure things out for themselves.

2. He is feeling the need to move beyond where he is, and yet he feels you pulling him back. He loves you, but he is trying to figure out a different way or different level of love for you—as a man, not as a boy. He can feel you making it harder for him to move forward (albeit unintentionally), which adds to his struggle. As a result he may be short with you, be irritated when you keep pressing him, or avoid your calls altogether.

3. He may have transitioned into a man more than you realize. He sees himself as a "grownup," and he wants you to see him this way, too. Setting boundaries, deciding where and how often he has contact

with you, and making decisions you are not happy with is not so much about you as it is about who he is now as a man. It is his way of letting you know things are different now. His priorities are not your priorities.

He sees his wife and children as his family, and so these are the people on whom he is focused and whom he sees as his priority. It's not that you aren't important, but your role in his life is not at the top of his priority list—the top spot belongs to his wife and children. He doesn't love you *less*, he just loves you *differently*. He wants you to see that his priorities have changed. He wants you to respect him and appreciate the man he has become.

As your son moves through this process, you need to let go more and more. Instead of taking the lead and behaving with him as you always have, which is typical for a parent, it's now more appropriate to sit back, watch, and listen. Let your son lead. Let him tell you where he is in his process through his actions. You need to make sure you pay attention and adjust your own expectations and behaviors accordingly.

There are also times, however, when a son may feel the need (albeit unconsciously) to take a more extreme measure to separate from his mother. This approach typically surfaces when a son and his mother have been close and his mom is (in his eyes) incredibly powerful. Her thoughts, ideas, and suggestions are so commanding and influential to him that he does not feel strong enough to push them (and her) away on his own. So his way of dealing with this may be to choose a spouse who, due to her style, personality, and personal issues, sets the tone for him to distance himself from his family, which then allows him to individuate and gain a sense of self. His wife is the one who moves him through his developmental process instead of him doing it himself, which means that whatever unfolds is now based on her needs, wants, and desires—not his. Not surprisingly, this situation is usually unhealthy for both of them—and for the MIL, as well.

## The DIL's Part

Even though a son's moving away emotionally and psychologically is part of his developmental process, sometimes the DIL *is* the reason that the distance between a son and his mother seems bigger than his mother thinks it should be. Some DILs struggle (often unknowingly) within themselves, which shows in their actions, particularly toward their husband's family—and the MIL specifically. A DIL's actions may have little or nothing to do with anything the MIL has actually said or done, but the DIL's perception is that the MIL has done some egregious act that warrants pushing her MIL away or banning her altogether.

Although this kind of behavior on the part of your DIL can feel as though it has happened out of the blue, it typically hasn't. It has happened for a reason. You may not *agree* with the reason. Heck, you may not even *know* the reason, but believe me, regardless of whether it is valid or not, there *is* a reason. You may also feel you have done everything you can think of to turn things around with her, but nothing seems to change—except that her anger toward you seems to be growing, which leaves you in a state of panic, fear, and anguish.

How your DIL responds or reacts to you is dependent on her own life experiences and personal history. These aspects will define how she shows her need to distance herself from you and pull her husband—your son—away even more than he would pull away on his own. Here are some examples of a few of the more problematic types of DILs (explained more thoroughly in my previous book, *Reluctantly Related* ) and how this behavior might manifest:

* Doubting Donna often feels as though her MIL is too motherly, which translates into her feeling as though her MIL is too intrusive, controlling, and smothering. Donna longs for a sense of family that she never really had, even though what she is longing for seems to be what she has with her own family. Due to this strong (often unconscious) desire, Donna works overtime to create this sense of "family" between her, her husband, their

children, and her family of origin (which is her way of trying to resolve some of her issues with them). In this sense, her MIL is a threat—not because the MIL did anything, but more because the MIL is simply not part of the DIL's family of origin, so she's not part of the dynamic the DIL is trying to heal. (Again, Donna may not be completely aware of these issues, or she may not be connecting them to her family of origin.)

As a result, Donna will likely focus more on her own family of origin and want her husband and their children to spend most, if not all, of their social time with them. She will have a tendency to exclude her MIL from typical grandparent things (such as babysitting, holidays, and so on) in lieu of including her parents, particularly her mother. These actions are a direct result of some unresolved issues the DIL has with her mother. It's also important to understand that if she allows herself to create this sense of family with her in-laws *without* resolving her issues with her mother, she would then "know" she never really had this sense of family with her family of origin—and this would be unthinkable!

- Weird Wendy typically finds her MIL's actions, regardless of what the MIL does or doesn't do, as "against" her. She will not only exclude her MIL from the typical grandparent events, but Wendy will also exclude her from most everyday activities, as well. She will make no effort to include her MIL in anything and will ignore the MIL's attempts to interact with her. The only *real* reason for doing this is that Wendy doesn't want to have to have anything to do with her husband's family. From Wendy's perspective, if her MIL is "against" her, she feels justified in excluding her.

It's important to keep in mind that even though Wendy does this with her MIL, she has often done the same thing with her own family. And she has probably made it difficult, if not impossible, for her husband to socialize outside of the people she "chooses" for them.

## The MIL's Part

Looking at what is going on in these situations with your DIL through an adult-to-adult perspective (rather than from a parent-to-child perspective) helps you shift your focus to where it needs to be: realizing that you are dealing with an adult, not a child, and definitely not *your* child. And when dealing with this adult, remember to focus on the bigger picture, asking yourself, *Is it more important for me to be right, or for me to have a relationship with my son, my DIL, and my grandchildren?* This seems like an easy question, but when you also feel wronged and hurt, you can lose sight of this. You can focus too much on wanting your DIL to understand your pain or on correcting what you believe to be your DIL's misperception.

Unfortunately, it is all too easy to get stuck in this place of feeling hurt, angry, and completely misperceived. And when you feel this way, you also feel justified in telling your friends, family, or anyone who will listen how unappreciative, selfish, childish, or even crazy your DIL is for the way she treats (or mistreats) you. It is much easier to keep the focus on how wrong your DIL is and on all the things she does that prevent you from having a relationship with your son and grandchildren.

But all that merely keeps you stuck where you are—in all the pain, heartache, and helplessness. Remember, it doesn't matter if your DIL is right or wrong. What matters at this moment is her perception. If you stay focused on the fact that you see her to be completely off base and so you believe you're justified in feeling wronged by her, you hurt yourself more than anything that your DIL could do or say to hurt you. You will be keeping yourself from getting what you really want—time with your son and grandchildren, and maybe even time with your DIL, too.

The only way to change your situation and have your son, grandchildren and yes, even your DIL in your life, is to learn the reason your DIL has pushed you out of the picture and then work from there. Regardless of who your DIL is—whether she's a Doubting Donna or a Weird Wendy—at this moment, she sees that you have wronged her in some way or maybe wronged them as a family. To begin the healing process, it's critical that you get to the bottom of things.

I know this is going to sound one-sided, but please bear with me for just a few minutes and hear me out before you completely dismiss what I'm saying. It is important to keep in mind that it doesn't matter if you believe or "know" what she is saying is wrong. Trying to change her mind and have her believe that her perception is wrong—that you didn't do or say whatever it is she says you did or said—will not happen. More times than not, it doesn't happen with anyone. And even though it may be one-sided and you're thinking, *What about me?* remember the bigger picture. Having your family in your life takes precedence over your hurt feelings—at least for the moment.

One of you has to break the stalemate to begin changing the relationship between you and your DIL. One of you has to put her feelings aside to get the dialogue rolling. Why not let that person be you? Once your DIL feels heard and you've moved past this blockage, a point may come where you will be able to share what was really going on for you so that you can set the record straight. It just can't be at this moment.

## More on the DIL

If you've read *Reluctantly Related*, then you know that there are other types of DILs besides just Doubting Donna and Weird Wendy. You may be wondering, *Where does Transitioned Tracy fit into this situation?* I did not include Transitioned Tracy in the part about the DIL pulling her husband away from his family because unlike Doubting Donna and Weird Wendy, Transitioned Tracy does not feel as though her MIL has done some egregious act. Tracy instead remains detached with no real sense or need to involve herself in whether or not she and her husband spend time with his family, particularly his mother. Tracy will often let her husband take the lead on when to include his family and how often. If he does not make an effort, she is likely to let things slide and not feel the need to pick up the slack for him.

This detachment that Transitioned Tracy projects can sometimes feel to a MIL as though her DIL doesn't really like her. This is really not the case. While to the MIL, it seems that Tracy makes no effort for "them" to spend time with her, in reality Tracy is following her husband's lead. He is the one who is making no effort, while the only role Tracy plays is in not bringing her husband's lack of familial effort to his attention and pushing for something more. (See *Reluctantly Related* for more explanation on Transitioned Tracy and the relationship this DIL type has with her MIL.)

## Having a DIL vs. a "Daughter"

How many times have you said, "I thought my daughter-in-law would be like a daughter to me"? Or maybe you didn't say that, but you just *hoped* it would be true. Even if you never actually expected that your DIL would call you "mom," you may instead have had an expectation of her now being "one of your children." *Now that my son is married,* you thought, *I not only have a son, but I also have a "daughter."* It seems natural.

Although this concept may have worked in past generations, today it is a misconception—and often a dangerous assumption. It's dangerous because that assumption can quickly and easily create a wedge or even a wall between you and your DIL.

Let's think about this for a minute. Your son is your child. He grew up around you. He knows your quirks, your moods, and when you are joking and when you are not. He knows you say things that (to be honest) do not always come out the way you want. He has figured out when to sit up and take notice and when to ignore you. The two of you have history together. It is the history you share that allows you both to overlook things, disagree, say what's on your mind, and then come back together—no harm, no foul. It is this history that allows your family members to have more leeway with their words and actions than anyone else.

The different types of MILs (also discussed in *Reluctantly Related*) will show this motherly inclination differently. Here are some examples:

- Mothering Margaret believes that treating her DIL as if she is one of her children shows love and acceptance of her DIL. To a certain degree, she accepts her son as an adult, but she still has the tendency to play the part of "mom." To Margaret, she is just being helpful when she steps in to do things around their house, buy things for them that she feels they "need," or gives her opinion about something they are planning to do, buy, and so on. To her DIL, Margaret's "helpful" actions can feel controlling, intrusive, and a bit too much like a "mom."

  When Margaret shares her thoughts and opinions with both her son and DIL, she does so as if she is talking to her "children." It may not be *what* she says, but more her tone of voice or even her body language that come across differently from the way she intended. This motherly tendency is also reflected in her expectations of her son and DIL. She often thinks, *Look at all I do for my son and his wife, and yet she doesn't appreciate any of it. She treats me as if I don't matter at all.*

- Off-the-Wall Wanda often feels as though her son should give her priority status over her DIL. She sees her role as the "mother" and her DIL's role as one who should listen, follow, and acquiesce. After all, this is what everyone around her seems to do, so why would it be different with her DIL?

  Wanda feels threatened by the importance her DIL has in her son's life. She will stop at nothing to regain the power and influence she feels she is entitled to with her son. She will say, do, and behave in any way she feels is necessary to get what she wants. The more she feels she is not in control, the more anxiety she experiences, and the more ramped up her actions will become. In other words, the more anxious she becomes, the more outrageous her actions get.

- Uncertain Sara struggles with where she fits into the world of her son and DIL, so she often comes across as giving mixed messages. One minute she may be too motherly (in other words, overstepping her boundaries), and the next minute she comes across as distant, unavailable, and maybe even a bit aloof.

For Sara's DIL, this is a bit confusing because Sara will indicate she wants to be involved in their lives, but not on a consistent basis. In fact, her DIL is never sure which version of Sara—the one who wants to be involved or the one who is more aloof—is going to show up at any given time.

It's important to remember when your son marries that he is not bringing home a daughter to you. He is bringing home an adult woman— someone with *her own* history, *her own* life experiences, and *her own* understanding of how she wants "family" to be. It's not that her way is right—it's that her way is *different*. Unlike your son, she does not know your quirks or your moods. She does not know when you are joking and when you are not. She may not be comfortable ignoring what you say or do or even know when she should. She takes what she sees and hears and filters them through her own family history experience.

## Action Steps

*For MILs:*

- Rate on a scale of 1–10 how much you have emotionally let go of your son, with 1 meaning you haven't let go at all and 10 meaning you have successfully let him go, creating a healthy relationship between the two of you. (Be willing to look at yourself honestly.)

- Describe how feeling less important in your son's life has affected you.

- Name some behaviors you display that could be interpreted by your DIL as being too motherly.

*For DILs:*

- Describe what you might be doing to push you and your husband further away from his family. (Be willing to look at your actions as honestly and objectively as possible.)

*For both MILs and DILs:*

- Describe how you might be placing the responsibility for the negative things in your relationship between you and your in-law squarely on your in-law. Consider what specific things you can do to change this.

# CHAPTER 8

# Growing Up Is Hard to Do

*Letting go is a two-way street, but if one person can't
do it, then it's up to the other to show the way.*

AS I MENTIONED IN CHAPTER 7, it is critical for mothers to let go
of their children and allow them to grow into who they are meant
to be. This is true not only for mothers and their sons, but also for
mothers and their daughters. Many MILs who also have daughters, as
well as the DILs I've talked to, really seem to have a problem with
this concept. They all shared their rationale, justifying why it is okay
for mothers and daughters to be really close, or in this case,
too close. What they often don't understand is that there's a
difference between having a close, healthy relationship and
being *too* close.

Erin and her mother are a perfect example of a relationship that is too close. When she came to see me, Erin told
me that she and her mother talk on the phone every day, or almost
every day, but that the conversations weren't necessarily long. When I
asked her what they typically talk about, Erin beamed. "We talk about
anything and everything," she said. "I share with my mom what is
going on in my life and she shares the same with me."

As she went into detail about the relationship, it became clear that they each share a great deal of intimate, emotional details with the other. "Of course I tell her about the kids and what is going on in their lives," Erin explained, "but I also talk with her about things that are troubling me, and she always helps me sort through my feelings. I'll ask her opinion about what's happening with the kids and I'll share my frustrations with the kids' teachers and other parents. We talk about issues going on between my husband and me, and I also talk to her about my MIL. We talk about whatever seems relevant at the time."

I then asked Erin how often she sees her family, and if it's just her mom or the entire family she usually gets together with. After some thought, Erin said, "We spend most holidays with my family. I just feel more comfortable around them, and my husband doesn't seem to mind—or at least he hasn't said anything to indicate he has an issue with it. Also, my mom volunteers whenever I need a sitter, which is great. It's just one less thing I have to worry about. She really makes things easier for me."

To some of you, what Erin describes may seem typical for a mother/daughter relationship. In fact, you might say, "They're close. So what's the problem?" Yes, their relationship is close—but it's *too* close. Their closeness comes at too great a cost. To determine that, I asked myself two basic questions:

1. How does Erin's relationship with her mother negatively impact Erin's other relationships—namely, with her husband, her MIL, her sisters-in-law, her own siblings, her friends, and so on?

2. How does this way of relating to one another affect Erin's developmental growth?

It's fairly obvious how challenges in a mother/daughter relationship can spill over into your relationships with others. But when you and your mother have a "close" relationship, it is much harder to see how this could be anything but positive—for everyone. So let's look at why this can be the case.

## Daughters Who Don't Grow Up

One of the most all-encompassing issues that arises with a "too close" relationship is that the daughter is not able to emotionally grow and mature in the way she needs to in order to become an adult. Before I go any further, let me first give you a universal example of how we all, at one time or another, have slid back into child-like roles without realizing we're doing so.

You have lived on your own for a while now, feeling pride in your maturity, individuality, and your ever-growing sense of adulthood. You feel you've learned to handle difficult situations and unsettling emotions in mature, rational ways. And you also love figuring things out, making your own decisions, and reaping the benefits of those decisions.

You are excited to be going home to visit your parents. Although you maintain phone contact with them, you haven't seen them in a while. You show up at your parents' house, toss your bags on the floor, and plop into the nearest chair. You smell the aroma of your favorite dinner cooking. Your mother is busy pulling food out of the refrigerator, asking you what you'd like to eat. You indulge her. She makes you a snack and you happily eat it. Being with your parents again feels so comfortable. It feels like *home*.

Throughout the long weekend, you find yourself chatting with your mother, eating, relaxing, and generally enjoying a sense of lavish indulgence. It feels great! You don't have a care in the world while you are there. It's wonderful having your mom take care of you. And on some level, you not only want this experience (and maybe expect it), but you also relish it, allowing your mother to do more and more for you. Although you hadn't really thought about it, you realize that this is what you love about being around your family—this sense of being taken care of in the way only *family* can do.

As great as this may feel, unknowingly you've set yourself up to revert to old roles and patterns. That sense of being taken care of, as good as it feels, puts you in a child-like role with your family. Mom lets you just hang out while she does all the things she did when you were younger. She allows you to take on the child role so that she can be in her mom role—the mom who took care of you. Both you and your mom are getting an emotional need met by allowing yourselves to be in this specific parent-child role again.

Now you may be thinking to yourself, *Why is this such a problem? It's not hurting anyone, and when I leave, I go back to my adult world.* In this particular situation, you probably will. And eventually—as you grow older and move through your developmental maturation—you will find that these old roles and patterns begin to subside when you go home. You move into a different emotional place as you mature. As a result, your expectations of the visit change, and your role with your mother (and father) during these visits changes from a parent-child role to an adult-adult role (and eventually to an adult-child role, with you becoming more of the caretaker with your parents).

Even so, this example shows you how easy it can be to fall back into child-like feelings and emotions, expectations, and behaviors. Getting stuck in this child-like way of thinking, feeling, and behaving can also occur when you have so much contact with your family (particularly your mother) that you are not able to move out of this mode (nor do you want to). With the constant contact between you and your mother, you simply can't get the distance you need to mature properly. You are constantly pulled back into the child-like place. And even though you may *like* being pulled back because it feels good, the truth is that you are really stuck in an unhealthy place.

## Hiccups with Your Husband

This "closeness" you feel when you talk to your mom daily (or almost every day) and share personal or even intimate details about your marriage or your relationships is really about recreating that feeling of being wrapped up, albeit emotionally, in your mom's arms and feeling secure, safe, and loved. But what happens to the other relationships in your life when you are emotionally wrapped up in your mother's arms?

Children don't have many expectations placed on them. Their responsibilities to others are minimal. Appropriately so, children are all about their own needs getting met instead of meeting the needs of others. But when you return emotionally to this dynamic, there's no room left for you to be an adult with your spouse, in-laws, siblings, friends, and so on.

Your behavior is going to reflect where you are emotionally. You will likely feel that these people are putting expectations on you that are not realistic. You and your husband may fight more about these expectations because he does not understand why you see them as unfair. You may get upset with him because you feel he is not taking care of you in the way you want or need. You may think, *Why doesn't he understand that his mom is wanting* too *much?* Or *Can't he see that his family is demanding too much of me—and of us? I'd rather be with my own family; at least they let me be me!* Another possibility is that your husband will say nothing, instead indulging you where you are in this child-like place. This, unfortunately, keeps you even more stuck in a place that not only hurts your relationships with others, but, in the end, also greatly hurts you.

I know this may be hard to hear, but this is not a normal, healthy state for an adult woman. In all fairness, though, you probably are not doing this on purpose. You probably did not realize the impact that staying this emotionally connected to your mother could have on you. You most likely thought you and your mother were just close—not too close. So what you want to think about now is, *Do I* really *want my relationship with my mother to prevent me from having healthy adult relationships with my husband and his family, or can I have a different relationship with my mother that better meets my needs now?*

Another issue that arises when you overshare concerns, problems, or issues about your husband or about your marriage with your mother is that you are providing her (and maybe the rest of your family) with a one-sided view of the situation. This is natural, of course, but your mother and other family members have a vested interest in you because you are their child or sibling. They feel the pain this situation is causing you, which taints their perspective. They do not want to see you hurting and so they will view your husband as "the bad guy." Now they have a skewed perspective of him.

You may get over your emotional upset. In fact, now that you have had the chance to vent, you may actually feel *much* better about your husband. But your mother and family members will not get over it as easily. They will tend to continue viewing your spouse in this negative light, a view that can unfortunately linger for a long time—sometimes forever—because they can't let go of what you've told them. They might even get upset with you because you seem to have forgiven him when they have not!

Yet another danger is that this oversharing can also give you a *temporary* sense of relief because the issue you were so upset about is actually still there. The person with whom you *should* have shared to actually resolve the problem or issue—your spouse—doesn't know you were upset, and so he is not in a position to help resolve the issue. Therefore, you leave the door wide open to having the problem arise again...and again...and again. When issues are not resolved, problems build and build until they loom so large that they *feel* unfixable, and thus they *become* unfixable.

## Your Mother vs. Your MIL

Another problem being "too close" to your family can cause is that the loyalty you feel for them can override all your other relationships. How can you let yourself enjoy the time with your MIL, sisters-in-law, and maybe even friends if you feel that by doing so you are being disloyal to those that matter so much to you—your mom and other family members? Look at this scenario:

You do something fun with your MIL and really enjoy your time with her. While talking to your mother, you innocently share this experience with her. Without actually acknowledging this to yourself, you sensed your mother pull back ever so slightly and get a little quiet. Your intuition tells you that something just happened, although you can't put your finger on exactly what it was.

The mood in the air seems to have changed. Without realizing it, you react to what you sensed in your mother. Now when you are with your MIL, you start to find her behaviors irritating, annoying, and maybe even smothering. You find reasons not to spend time with her. You may even look for things about her that drive you crazy so that you create a wedge between the two of you—and all of this occurs under the surface, without your full awareness. After all, it's easier to find fault with your MIL and to push her away than it is to lose that closeness with your mother.

Oversharing with your mother about what upsets or irritates you about your MIL can also sabotage your relationship with your in-law. Here is what can happen:

You just spent a few days with your MIL and now you are tired, stressed, and uncertain about what to do with the way you're feeling. Your mother happens to call, and you give her a blow-by-blow account of your weekend with your MIL. Your mother reaffirms that you are justified in feeling the way you do. She reinforces what you've been saying about your MIL from the beginning—that *she's crazy!* She says all the things you want (and need) to hear to feel better about yourself and justified in how you feel. You now feel empowered! You then act on this new sense of authority and power.

And then your mother quietly asks you why you put up with the way your MIL treats you. She doesn't say it directly, but she implies that you don't need people in your life who treat you this way or who make you feel bad about yourself. You listen, all the while merging your feelings of empowerment with this new awareness.

When you share with your mother issues or concerns you have with your MIL, again, she is hearing only one side of the story. And again, she has a vested interest in protecting you. However, your mother may have her own agenda as well. To some extent, your MIL is her competition for your time and attention, as well as for the grandchildren. She may not say this, but it is true: Your mother (and your MIL) both want to see you and your family as often as they can. They want to spend as much time with the grandchildren as possible.

Your mother's connection with you slants things in her favor, and let's be honest, sharing is not always easy. Now I'm not saying this is *always* what is going on, but I am saying that it is one possible consequence of being "too close" to your mother. After all, it's hard for *anyone* to avoid having their own agenda. And remember, in a "too close" relationship, both you and your mother are getting your emotional needs met. You're each exerting as much of a pull as the other to maintain the parent-child relationship.

## Unhealthy Dependency

Another way to look at this is that having this close of a "connection" with your mother causes you to develop a certain dependency. Because your mother is the authority figure, this increases the dependency even more and reinforces the parent-child roles you fall in to. This emotional dependency is often subtle because it's so easy to explain it away. ("My mother is my best friend." "I can always share what is going on with her." "She gets me in a way no one else does.")

Well, of course she gets you. She raised you. She knows you like a mom knows her child. However, you are now a grown woman who is married and may even have children of her own. As an adult, you need to be formulating your own thoughts, ideas, and beliefs about yourself and about your family. You need to be figuring out—with your spouse—what *your* family will look like. It cannot be a carbon copy of your mother's life or of your MIL's life. It cannot be a carbon copy of *your* life growing up or your *husband's* life as he grew up. It will be what the *two of you* create together.

Further, when you share so much with your mother and maintain that parent-child connection, you are excluding other people from being a part of your familial experience—people who deserve to be part of your emotional associations. By expanding your emotional world to include other people, you are not excluding your mother. You're just widening your emotional network. Trust me, there's enough room for everyone.

Because both mothers and daughters are getting some of their emotional needs met by the other, it can be hard for either of them to let go. Holding on feels good to both of you. Although mothers should be the ones to show their daughters how to do this, it's often difficult when the daughters don't want to let go. That tugs at a mother's heart because it makes her feel needed and loved. However, just like mothers of sons, mothers of daughters need to find other areas where they can get these needs met. Or better yet, they need to find a sense of identity that better fits where they are at this point in their lives. Their role as mother—as the caretaker and nurturer— needs to change as their daughters mature and grow into the women they were meant to be.

## Action Steps

- Reflect honestly on your relationship with your mother.

    o How close is it?

    o In what ways might it be "too close"?

- How does your relationship with your mother impact your relationships:

    o With your spouse?

    o With your MIL?

    o With your other in-laws?

    o With your siblings?

- What can you do differently to allow other people to be included rather than excluded?

# CHAPTER 9

# The Man (or Son) in Your Life

*When we allow a man to show us how he is different*
*from us, we not only have an opportunity to embrace*
*those differences, but we also strengthen our*
*relationship with him.*

I HAVE TALKED A BIT ABOUT HUSBANDS and sons in previous chapters to help MILs and DILs better understand what their son or spouse are experiencing when it comes to separating, but not removing, himself from his family of origin (particularly from his mother). Now I'd like to provide some insight into who this man is, what he brings to the MIL/DIL relationship, and what he can do to help his wife and mother adjust to their new roles as in-laws.

As I discussed in *Reluctantly Related,* several different male person-alities come into play within the different MIL/DIL relationships. Even though these men are quite different in their characteristics and their approach to the MIL/DIL relationship, they still share certain things in common with each other as men.

We already know that men think and act in ways that are different from women, but in most cases, women don't fully understand these differences from a psychological perspective. And while that perspective can sometimes be confusing and even frustrating to comprehend, doing so is the key to happier and more fulfilling relationships—not only with the men in our lives, but also with our in-laws. Let me explain.

As a man moves out of childhood into adulthood, he begins to make some small changes in how he relates to his family. Yes, a son still calls home and talks to his mother and his father, but what they may not pay a whole lot of attention to is that *how* he talks to each parent is changing.

When he's talking to his mother, a son still feels the pull to call often, share much, and remain who he has always been—her child. And in all honesty, whether right or wrong, a son tries to accommodate this to some extent. He may try to call a little less often and share a little less, but he feels this tug to maintain the status quo, which makes emotionally pulling away difficult. Because mothers want to maintain that sense of family—as it has always been—their sons often feel torn between wanting to show respect to their mothers in this way and feeling the need to emotionally separate.

A father, on the other hand, has moved into a different relationship with his son. Yes, he talks to his son on the phone or when he visits, but he doesn't worry about how often the two of them connect. A dad respects his son for having his own nuclear family and now sees his son as the head of that family. He knows he will talk with his son when it happens. He feels a bond with his son regardless of whether they talk once a week or once a month.

Because a father is also a man, he understands (often without even realizing it) what his son is experiencing and what his son needs to grow into the man he is meant to be. A father understands that his son needs to find his own way. He identifies with his son's need to establish himself as a man. He knows what it is for a man to love a woman, to want to protect her and provide for her. He appreciates his son's desire to create *his* family and be who his wife and children need him to be, as well as who he wants to be for *them*. A father gets what it is to be a man, and so he willingly gives his son the space he knows his son needs.

As you can see, there's a huge difference between how a mother experiences this process and how a father experiences it. A mother feels the pain of loss, while the father understands his son's journey. No one talks about what is going on, which is why this can be a painful, confusing, and easily misunderstood experience for the various people going through it. Both parents may even struggle between themselves during their son's process, due to how each one is experiencing their son's developmental maturation.

It is difficult for a man to explain to his wife what "being a man" is all about, including what he goes through to get there and what he needs to help him along the way. So when a father sees his wife in pain, hurting because their son no longer behaves as he once did, he is torn between wanting his son to maintain the status quo so his wife feels better and not really knowing how to explain to his wife what is going on with their child. And so he stands back and watches, often letting things play out.

## Gender Differences

We are all aware of the many differences between how boys behave and how girls behave. For example, you might see this difference in their energy levels, their types of play, the way they interact, and so on. One example of how boys handle interactions differently from girls has to do with how boys handle problems with their friends.

Think back to grade school, middle (or junior high) school, or even high school. When girls get upset with their friends, they typically tell other friends about their grievances, stirring the pot and holding on to their hurt or angry feelings for a really long time. In other words, they take things personally and will bring other people into the situation even if those people have no knowledge of what actually transpired. And girls can hold on to these hurt feelings for days, weeks, years, and sometimes forever. Girls also expect their confidants to be loyal to them by continuing to shun or snub the person who wronged their friend.

Boys, on the other hand, handle issues with friends differently. They may have a few choice words with each other, they may even physically hit or fight one another, but within a short period of time, they are over whatever it was that upset them. And then they're usually still friends with one another. They let it go. This can happen within minutes or hours, depending on how old they are and what caused the rift. They don't feel the need to share the specifics of what occurred with their other friends, and so they don't ask or expect their other friends to take sides.

Now, I am not saying one of these ways is right and the other is wrong, but what *is* important is recognizing that there are indeed differences between how the genders behave. Girls take things personally and hold a grudge—while boys do not. And these differences continue from childhood into adulthood. Women still take wrongs or slights personally and hold grudges, where men do not. Women still involve other people in their relationship difficulties for support—and they insert themselves into other people's relationships, including their children's marriages or in-law issues—where men do not.

This is extremely important when you think about how we, as women, get upset with our spouses or the other men in our lives when they do not understand how someone wronged us. They don't get that we hang on to our hurt feelings, particularly when it's a MIL or a DIL who we feel has done us wrong.

And although we women often want men to be more like us when it comes to relationships, we need to appreciate that a man's way of handling such situations isn't necessarily all bad. In fact, maybe we could learn something from how they look at relationships and add it to our mental and emotional repertoire.

## The Power of Women

At times, it may not seem or feel like it, but from a man's perspective, women play a dominant role in their lives and in their hearts. This dominance can be positive or negative, or some combination of the two. It can also be positive at one point in a man's life and negative at another point, depending on the circumstances.

This dominance can be in the form of love, a sense of power, a need to control him, or again, some combination of these. For example, as a young boy this dominance is often in the form of love, which is understandable because the woman in his life—his mother—plays a major role for him. She is "mom." She nurtures, loves, and cares for him in a way no one else does. Her love and acceptance is critical to his survival and his sense of self-worth.

What I've learned from men is that as a boy grows up, he has a deep respect, as well as a deep fear, of the central female figure in his life—beginning with his mother and later shifting to his wife. In fact, there's an ongoing balancing act between the respect and the fear he feels for this central female figure. He appreciates, values, and honors who this woman is, but he also fears her disapproval, her disrespect, and her ultimate rejection. And as he moves through the process of shifting this respect from his mother to his wife, his fears of disapproval, disrespect, and rejection may now involve either his mother or his wife—or both women.

For example, when a DIL is upset with her husband's mother and instead of dealing with her MIL directly, tells her husband, "You need to say something to your mother about this situation," it packs a one-two punch. First, one of the two most powerful women in his life is asking him to confront or challenge the other most powerful woman. Yikes! Second, because this is not *his* fight, he doesn't have any real conviction behind the issue, and that means that even if he does say something to his mother, he doesn't really get why he is saying it. The MIL often senses this lack of conviction, which sends a confusing message to her.

Besides a son experiencing dominance through love, he can also experience it through a sense of power—as in his mother being in a position of power over him. Usually, as he grows older, his mother's power gradually diminishes to a point where the son can naturally separate from his mother and mature, growing into his own person. But sometimes the dominance he feels from his mother can be so powerful that it leaves him feeling powerless.

This does not mean that his mother is domineering or controlling (although it *could* mean that). What it does mean is that the bond or connection that the son has with his mother is so strong that he *feels* the power of that connection and is unsure how to deal with it as he gets older. As a child, the feeling is comforting and loving, yet as an adult, this bond can feel stifling—and then he feels immobilized because this strong bond makes separation difficult. The very nature of his mother's words or actions looms over him, which reinforces his own sense of powerlessness. So what is this man to do? How can he separate when he feels so powerless?

When a son feels this vulnerable or incapable of separating through the more direct, natural way, he often unconsciously chooses to do so through an indirect method. For example, he may marry a woman who will "help" him with this separation. She will be a woman who is so different from his family that there is likely to be friction and tension from the onset. His wife will dictate—and he will allow her to dictate—the terms of his relationship with his family. Whether she does this through being strong herself or by being needy, he may also join her in the pushback she gives his family when his family tries to involve him in their lives.

Unfortunately, his wife typically does so based on her own unresolved issues with her parents or family. And thus, a MIL starts to see that she is being left out of everything, whereas her DIL's family may be invited or encouraged to participate in everything they do. Sometimes the husband's family is totally removed from his life altogether—which also means his children are removed from their paternal grandparents' lives. Here is an example of just such a situation:

Karen describes her family as close when her children were growing up. Although both she and her husband worked when their kids were young, their schedules were flexible, so they had ample time to be involved with their kids and their activities. Her two oldest children were close in age, so they spent a fair amount of time together. But for various reasons having to do with what else was going on in the family at the time, Karen spent more time with her youngest child, Tom. Although he had the most easy-going personality of the three children, Karen still was under the impression that the whole family got along really well. She *thought* they had a great family.

But once her children became adults, things with Tom were different. He became distant, and Karen didn't understand what was going on with him. He didn't even introduce his family to his girlfriend Meredith until after they were engaged. His parents didn't have any idea he was seeing anyone special. So suddenly finding out Tom was getting married was a bit of a shock to Karen.

"I don't see what he sees in her," Karen told a friend. "She is rude, distant, and at times antagonistic. It wasn't until Meredith came into the picture that Tom started to find fault with everything we do—especially with everything *I* do! It's as if I had been the worst parent in the world."

She then began relating how distant Tom had become and the nasty comments he would make to her and to his father. He seemed to find reasons not to include them in his life, and soon—with a new grandchild on the way—the situation was devastating to Karen.

If you look at the situation I just described, you can see that Tom likely feels unable to emotionally break away from his family, and his actions show how he unconsciously chose to handle his developmental maturational process. He and his mother were always close. This may have been because he is more like her than he is like his father. Tom may have felt that he had been in everyone else's shadow—his siblings' shadow as well as his parents' shadow—most of his life. Or maybe he didn't feel that he was as worthy as his siblings (or father), or maybe he felt some combination of these possibilities. Whatever the reason, Tom struggled to break away in a direct, clear manner.

His choice of a wife may have helped him to break away from his family of origin, but at a very high price. In this situation, choosing a woman to create the environment for breaking away sets up the husband's relationship with his family to be all or nothing—either he has contact with his family and continues to feel like a child, or he gets rid of them so he can be a man. On top of this, he has now replaced one woman with whom he *felt* overpoweringly dominated with another woman who *is* overpoweringly dominating.

Now I am not saying that this man is doomed or that his situation (or his mother's) can never change, because that is not true. Many times a man will reach a point in his life when he outgrows the need to keep his family at bay in order to be a man. He begins to realize that he can be a man, separate from his family of origin, and still have that family in his life. He comes into his own, feeling stronger and more grounded in his manhood.

Some of this internal growth occurs through his own life experiences, including exchanges in his marriage and his maturational process. And some of his growth is a direct result of his mother doing things a bit differently, showing him that he can be a man and still have a relationship with his parents and siblings. And although his mother can't control his part of this growth, she does have control over her part of it. She can begin to make some changes in how she relates to her son, changes that help him realize he *is* a man, and most importantly, she can help him realize that *she* sees her son as a man.

## Relationships and Priorities

Another aspect of a woman's influence is in the way a man views his relationships. Earlier in his life, his family (particularly his mother and father) play a major role in his concept of family. They are the cornerstone of what family means to him. However, once he starts a serious relationship with a woman and decides to marry, that concept of family begins to change. He shifts his idea of family away from his family of origin and onto himself and his wife. This relationship now takes priority over anything or anyone.

For a man, loving a woman includes an inherent need or desire to take care of her or provide for her. This is so not just financially, although that is an important component, but also physically, emotionally, and mentally. His job, in his eyes, is to make her his priority. A man wants more than anything for his wife to be happy, and he will often do whatever he can to make that happen. However, sometimes this is at the expense of his mother's feelings.

Here is an example:

Dawn is at a loss to understand what is going on with her son Tony and his wife Ann. They have been married only for a short time, but it seems as though they are spending less and less time with his side of the family, particularly on holidays. Dawn has tried to plan holidays so that Tony and Ann would be there with the rest of the family, but it never seems to work out that way.

"I've tried everything I can think of to get them to come for the holidays—at least one of the holidays—but there is always an excuse," she complains to her best friend. "They are willing to be here *before* or *after* the holiday, but never *on* the holiday. It just seems so unfair that they spend all their time with her side of the family. I've tried saying something to Tony about it, but he doesn't really respond."

In this situation, Dawn feels that her DIL is deciding for both Ann and Tony where they are going to spend the holidays, specifically deciding to spend all the holidays with Ann's family. And if Ann was like the DIL I described in Chapter 8 who is too close to her mother, then Dawn's perception of the situation may be accurate. However, this is not the only possibility. As I said previously, a husband's priority is his wife, and he will do what he can to make her happy.

In the situation with Tony and Ann, spending time with Ann's family is important to *her*, particularly on holidays. And for Tony, spending time with family on the holidays is not *as* important as it is to Ann. He loves his parents and siblings, but he views his wife as his family now. He enjoys seeing his parents, but seeing them on the actual holiday is less important to him than seeing them some time around the holiday, and it's definitely less important than his wife's happiness.

As difficult as this idea might be to accept, it is important for MILs to think about this as a possibility before jumping to the conclusion that their son's wife is the one who is calling all the shots. Do not assume that your son is at the mercy of his wife's whims. On the flip side, however, it is important for DILs to appreciate what it must feel like for their husband's side of the family to no longer have the holidays and other events as they have always been. And maybe, just maybe, this can soften a DIL's hard and fast idea of what being with family is all about.

## A Man's Role in the MIL/DIL Relationship

A man is in such a precarious situation when he marries. Whether he realizes it or not, he has two women who not only love him, but who are also vying for the influence they have over him. At first, these women don't really know each other, nor have they developed any kind of solid foundation with which to form a relationship. And yet, here he is and here these two women are, thrown together in hopes of the three of them forming some kind of comfortable connection with one another.

As much as we put the emphasis on the two women—the MIL and the DIL—the husband *does* play a role in their relationship. Often, he can make it easier for them to form a relationship. Now I am not saying he has *all* the power in that respect, because he doesn't, but what I *am* saying is that he can help the situation by doing his part. So what exactly *is* his part?

A man can often set the tone for the MIL/DIL relationship by how he handles himself when he interacts with his mother or talks with his wife. When he is clear about who he is, what his role as an adult is, and how important it is to communicate where he sees both women fitting into his world, the transition from being a single man to being a married man goes a lot easier—for all of them. His mother starts to see and accept that her role with her son is changing, and his wife is more at ease knowing she is his priority.

However, sometimes he is not able to make these things as clearly defined as he could, which makes this transition more difficult. This may be due to the husband's struggle to communicate what he really feels, it may be because his mother won't let go or doesn't realize she is still holding onto him, or maybe it's because of his wife's own insecurities getting in the way of her belief that she is his priority. And more often, it's some combination of all three. Here is an example of how the husband's struggle with communicating adds fuel to the fire when his wife's insecurities are a factor in the MIL/DIL relationship:

Robert and his mother were just about to hang up from a pleasant phone conversation when his mother said, "Robert, honey, I really could use your help. I've wanted to get these shelves up for some time now, but I can't do it myself. Would you help me?"

Robert was more than willing to help and agreed to come over Saturday morning. They agreed that he would come over around 10 a.m. and he figured he would easily be home by noon. After all, he knew his wife Ellen usually slept in on Saturday mornings and enjoyed relaxing a bit before starting the day. This would give her a chance to get up when she wanted and to have time to herself before he returned.

During dinner the following day, Robert mentioned to Ellen that he was going to stop by his mom's place on Saturday morning to put up some shelves for her. Ellen became quiet. When he asked her what was wrong, she couldn't stop herself. "Why do you always do that?" she asked. "I thought we were going to the nursery to get all the spring plants and flowers for the yard. We've been talking about it for weeks now. Your mom always does this! She knows the only time we really have together is on the weekends."

Robert was at a loss. He wasn't sure what had just happened. He knew they were planning to go to the nursery, but he thought they were going Saturday afternoon. Or at least he figured it wouldn't be until afternoon because Ellen sleeps in and relaxes Saturday mornings. He didn't know *this* Saturday would be any different.

Both Robert and Ellen are playing into the escalation of this scenario. Robert's part is his uncertainty with his ability to communicate with his mother and his wife about where he sees both women fitting into his world. Ellen's part is her own insecurities about herself and her place in her husband's life. Let me outline what happened in more detail:

Robert's role:

1. Robert did not communicate with his mother that, yes, he is willing to help her, but he wants to check with Ellen first to see what they have planned for Saturday. *This shows his mother he can be available to her, but Ellen is his priority.*

2. He did not communicate with Ellen what his reasoning was behind choosing Saturday morning to help his mother. He remembered that they were going to the nursery. But he thought they could go in the afternoon since he knows Ellen likes to sleep in and have a relaxing morning, and he figured he could give her a chance to do that before they started their day together. *This shows Ellen that he is being respectful of her and her Saturday routine, and it demonstrates that his willingness to help his mother is at his and Ellen's convenience.*

Ellen's role:

1. Ellen struggles with her overall self-worth, which colors her ability to see her husband's actions as a gesture of kindness toward her as opposed to a slight against her.

2. She chooses to ignore the fact that her actions—her ritual of sleeping in on Saturday mornings and moving into the day gradually—played a role in her husband's decision to go to his mother's house early. He wasn't taking anything away from his wife; he was basing his decision on his wife's routine.

As you can see, not only do Robert's and Ellen's actions affect *their* relationship, but those actions also affect the MIL/DIL relationship as well as Robert's relationship with his mother. Robert and Ellen are now at odds with each other, as another fight has broken out with his mother as the focal point. Ellen sees this as her MIL being demanding and taking her husband's time and attention away from her. Robert will now become more hesitant to agree to help his mother again and possibly even pull back from her to avoid further conflict with Ellen.

## What a Man Can Do

A man can help the MIL/DIL relationship by doing his part to move through his developmental maturational process. Whether he does this while he is still single or after he is married, his progress through this process allows both his mother and his wife (or future wife) to see that he is becoming or has become his own man. This alone will help both women feel less competitive with one another, which in turn allows them to see each other a bit more realistically. And it allows them to forge ahead, building a healthy relationship between the two of them instead of feeling as though each is trying to undermine the other.

Working through this developmental maturational process is a little more clouded when a man is already married, but even so, his willingness to communicate during this time plays a major role in his mother and his wife understanding what he is saying and why. Here are a few examples of how two different types of husbands show the struggle of separating and communicating:

- In-the-Middle Michael is still in the process of moving through his maturational process. Depending on where he is in this progression, he typically does not communicate with either his wife or his mother about why he is reacting or responding the way he does. He characteristically tries to placate both his mother and his wife because he doesn't feel comfortable taking a stand. However, when he does say something to either one of them, two challenging situations occur. First, by not being clear about why he is saying what he is saying, Michael allows his mother to believe that the idea or thought is coming from his wife. Second, Michael's lack of conviction or ability to take a stand on something causes his wife to feel threatened by what she fears is her MIL's influence over her husband (the MIL's son).

- Struggling Steven, on the other hand, has moved further through the maturational process than Michael, but he is not yet confident about how to express himself in order to make the fewest waves possible. He struggles with wanting acceptance and love, but to him, making waves goes against these two desires. So herein lies his dilemma: If Steven communicates more with his mother and his wife about what makes sense to him in relating as a family, this might initially create a wave or two, but in the long term it would clear the air and allow for better communication all around. But because Steven fears these waves would result in his being shunned by either his wife or mother—or worse, by both—he freezes and opts to avoid anything that will put the focus on him. This sets the stage for his mother to feel at a loss to know what to do, and it allows his wife to believe she is right to shun his family.

When a man communicates to his mother that what he is saying is *his* thought or *his* idea or that it is a joint decision that he is very much in agreement with, it sets a boundary for his mother to see. It helps her be clear about where this decision or thought is coming from. If he expresses himself, yet leaves things vague or avoids making it clear that the decision came from him, his mother will likely interpret his words in the way that feels most comfortable for her—which means blaming her DIL. It is easier for the MIL to put the blame on her DIL than it is to think her son is emotionally moving away or separating from her. This is when I hear MILs say things like, "He was never like this before he married her," or "We were so close until he got married," or sometimes even, "She won't *let* him see his family."

On the other hand, when a husband shares his thought process or logic with his wife, clarifying why he is saying or doing what he is saying or doing, he helps her understand what is behind his actions. Although she may not agree with what he says, she is less likely to misinterpret his actions as being what she *fears* to be true—fears that are attached to her insecurities and self-doubt, not to the truth.

## Action Steps

- Think about how the way you handle issues with friends and family differs from the way your husband handles issues with his friends and family. Then identify what effect, positive or negative, these differences have on your marriage.

- Make a list of the people you confide in about the issues you have with your husband. Describe how these discussions could negatively impact your relationship with that person as well as how they could negatively impact your marital relationship. (Describe something separate for each person you talk to.)

- Explore within yourself why you do not talk to your husband directly about the issues between the two of you. Ask yourself these questions:

  o What is your part in why you don't talk to him?

  o What is your husband's part in this situation?

  o What can *you* do to make talking together about your issues easier?

- Identify the ways you help your husband in shifting his respect and priority from his mother to you. Reflect on which of these ways are positive and on which may actually be negative.

# CHAPTER 10

# Marriage, MILs, and Mayhem

*Your experience as a couple should include growth, maturity, and eventually wisdom. How you choose to conduct yourself with each other and with family—both his and hers—is the true test of your love for one another.*

IN THE LAST TWO CHAPTERS, I talked about specific characteristics of the DIL (Chapter 8) and the husband/son (Chapter 9) that would help explain these individuals better, and I also discussed how these characteristics may affect the MIL/DIL relationship. But what happens when these two individuals become a couple? Being a couple is more complex than you might imagine, especially when you add the MIL into the mix. In this chapter, I'm going to explore how marital issues often get confused as MIL issues as well as give you some ideas you might not have considered before—ideas that once you understand them can help you in both your marriage and your MIL/DIL relationship.

## Marital vs. MIL Issues

Think about when you got married for a minute—you have two people who grew up in different families, with different emotional baggage, different values, different traditions, different ways of expressing themselves, different coping strategies, different...well, you get the picture. With all these different components coming into play, the marital relationship can be challenging enough. But when you add the relationship each is developing with the other's family, it can get even more challenging (to say the least). One of the major challenges for couples is when in-laws, particularly MILs, are involved in the couple's issues. What typically starts out as an issue the DIL has with her MIL (or vice versa) ends up becoming a couple's issue.

Here is an example:

It's happened again! Candice cannot take another situation with her MIL. "Why does she say those awful things to me?" she asks her husband Carl. "She has no respect for me, and yet she wants me to respect *her*."

"You know how she is," Carl starts to reply. "She's..."

"Why are you defending her?"

"I'm not! I'm just trying to tell you why she acts that way."

"I don't care *why* she acts that way; I just want her to stop!" A long awkward silence ensues. Candice waits for Carl to say something—something helpful, something supportive...*anything*—but he just sits there and says nothing. "Why don't you say something?" Candice pleads, her voice escalating, clearly exasperated because she has been in this situation before with Carl and she's tired of his unwillingness to deal with his mother.

Feeling Candice's rage, Carl continues to sit, paralyzed and panicked. If he wasn't sure what to say before, he is even less sure now. All he can think is, *Candice is not only mad at my mom, but now she's furious at me!*

The silence between Carl and Candice ends up lasting several days. This is not the first time this type of scenario has played out between them. Whenever his mother is an issue, they seem to fall right back into this same argument with one another. Eventually, they both settle down and move on, and things appear fine between them again. They appear to be back to where they were before this big blowup involving his mother occurred.

A few weeks later, Carl gets a phone call from his mother. "Carl, why don't you and Candice come by this weekend?" she asks. "Kevin and Barb will be in town and I thought we could have a family get-together," she says, mentioning Carl's brother and sister-in-law.

Carl is hesitant. He thinks about the blowup he and Candice had a few weeks ago, and he doesn't want a repeat of that. He knows Candice does not want to be around his mom. "Um, gee, I don't know, Mom," he stammers. "We have so much going on right now. I'll have to get back to you," knowing full well he won't call his mom back.

What is going on here? On the surface, especially to the players who are in the middle of the drama, it seems as though Carl's mom is causing problems for everyone. It looks like a MIL issue. But is it? Well, there *might* be a MIL issue, but more importantly, there appears to be a marital issue. What often starts out as a MIL/DIL issue can quickly move into a marital issue because like Carl and Candice, both you and your spouse have unspoken desires and expectations. When issues get compounded like this, neither the MIL/DIL issue nor the marital issue ends up getting resolved. More often than not, both issues become *worse.*

Not only are the husband's and wife's desires and expectations not the same, but often, neither the husband nor the wife have shared with the other what they want and how they see the situation. Couples usually do not spend much time talking about how they will interact with extended family, particularly both sets of in-laws (for example, how much time and in what circumstances they will interact with each other's parents, what that interaction will look like, where the in-laws fit in during holidays, what boundaries may need to be set, and so on). What often happens is the wife leads and the husband follows, with no real discussion about why they are doing what they are doing and how that may or may not work for the other. As I said in the last chapter, husbands want their wives to be happy, even if that is at their own expense—or the expense of the husband's family.

In many ways this puts a lot of the responsibility on the wife to create some kind of balance between the two families and the couple. And in that sense, it's not really fair for the husband to put his wife in that position. Women tend to lean toward spending more time with their own family because, of course, they are more comfortable with them. It is much more work to be with people with whom you didn't grow up and who don't know you the way your own family does. Although this is the way things may *usually* go, it does *not* mean it's the best option. In most cases, striking a balance between the desires and needs of the husband and wife as well as of both of the extended families is important.

Couples create a void when they don't talk honestly about what they each want or expect of one another as individuals *and* as a couple, or about what they expect of their extended families—not to mention of friends, work, money, and so on. The spouse's own desires and expectations naturally fill in this void, because he or she assumes *this must be okay with my spouse since they haven't said anything to contradict it.* And yet it rarely if ever is what the spouse had in mind.

For example:

Randy and Linda have been happily married for about five months. It seems they agree on everything. Linda can't think of a single argument they've ever had, and when asked, she and Randy both say, "We talk about everything."

Long before she got married, Linda had always envisioned that she and her future husband would do everything with her family—or at least a lot of things. She loved spending time with them, whether it was for vacations, birthdays, or even just getting together for a barbeque. Spending the holidays with her family was a given, of course. She couldn't ever imagine *not* doing that.

When she and Randy married, they talked about everything under the sun—everything except how they planned to include in-laws and extended family in their lives. Linda never even thought to talk to him about holidays at her parents' house or the subject of holidays at all for that matter. It never dawned on her that they'd need to discuss it. She just assumed what she had naturally envisioned would be what they'd do.

As the holidays neared, Linda and her mother were constantly on the phone making plans for the first holiday she and Randy would share as a married couple. When Randy overheard one of these conversations, he was stunned. As he listened, he kept thinking, *When did we decide we'd be going to her family's for the holiday?* He wasn't sure what to make of this, and he definitely wasn't sure what to do about it.

And so what happens when these unspoken expectations begin to surface? The wife gets angry and lashes out at her husband, expecting him to know why she is upset. Or she withholds and withdraws from him because she thinks he should know this is what she would or would not want. The husband tries to either rationalize what he is feeling or saying to his wife, or he shuts down completely, saying nothing and hoping he won't make things worse. How each spouse chooses to handle his or her frustration with the other and how each tries to resolve the issues between them demonstrates how serious their marital issues are.

Here is how the situation turned out for Linda and Randy:

Randy stewed for a bit over what he had overheard. He wasn't sure what to do, but he wasn't happy that Linda just assumed what their holiday plans were going to be. It felt to him as though he wasn't part of this equation at all, as though Linda and her mother were deciding his life. *I thought Linda was married to me*—not *her mom!* he said to himself. As upset as he was, Randy didn't want to upset Linda or have an argument with her, but he couldn't stop thinking about the situation. Finally, he decided to broach subject with her—or at least to test the waters.

"Linda, when did we decide we were spending the holidays with your family?" he said one evening after dinner. "I don't remember us talking about it." Linda was taken aback. She couldn't believe he was saying anything; after all, he had never said anything about the holidays, let alone his preference for how they would spend them.

"What are talking about?" she replied. "You *know* how important my family is to me, and since you never brought up the subject, I figured it didn't really matter to you. And since it *doesn't* matter to you and it *does* to me, I just figured we would spend the holiday with my family."

Randy wasn't sure what to say next. Linda's logic made little to no sense to him, but she seemed so strong in her conviction. He started to argue with her, but then stopped himself and thought, *Is it really worth the fight right now? Maybe this is something we can deal with later—after the holiday.*

But why does all this matter when you *know* it's your MIL who is causing the *real* problems? Well, not so fast! Before you can be successful in resolving the issues you have with your MIL, you have to address the issues in your marriage first. Without you and your husband being on the same page, supporting one another and working together, you will never resolve any of your MIL/DIL issues. And worse than that, focusing only on the MIL issues and not the marital issues will weaken your marriage.

So how do you know if you're fighting about a MIL issue or a marital issue? Here are some signs that the problem is a marital issue:

- You expect or want your husband to fix his mother or fix the problem.

- You start arguing about something his mother said or did, but then the fight expands to other issues between the two of you.

- You include such statements as "You always..." or "You never..." in your arguments.

- As you start talking about the issue you have with his mother, you become keenly aware of how much respect you are losing for your husband.

- The same issues keep surfacing, no matter how many times you argue about his mother.

- You want to cut off all ties to his side of the family.

- You feel anger toward him when he is hesitant to cut off his family or when he begrudgingly agrees to have less contact with them.

Again, addressing your marital issues first is necessary before you can begin to work on your MIL/DIL issues. But what happens when these issues seem to go hand-in-hand? Couples often say, "We don't really fight about anything but his mother." That may be true, but how you fight, as well as the way you resolve any conflict, is a reflection of how healthy your marriage is, not a reflection of your MIL/DIL issues.

So when you feel you have a problem with your MIL, you want to make sure that you are able to find a way to resolve it, not create World War III. And to do that, you need to make sure that any marital issues do not get in the way. Here are some strategies to help you keep things on the right track:

- **Figure out what you want from your husband.** Do you want to vent and have him just listen, to understand your emotional pain—or do you want something else? (Sorry, he cannot fix it for you.) It is important that you get clear on this first, because if *you* don't know what it is you want from him, how can *he* know?

- **Let him in on what you want early on.** Begin your conversation by letting him know up front what you want from him. How you word your request is critical to getting what you are after. If you are berating his mother or blaming him, you are *not* going to get what you want—even if venting makes you feel better.

- **Keep the focus on the two of you.** Remember, you are working on getting closer to your spouse right now so that the two of you can work together to find a resolution to whatever the MIL issue might be. His mother just happens to be the catalyst, so keep her out of it until you both feel okay about how you want to handle the situation with her.

## Setting Boundaries with Consequences

As adults, it seems odd that we may have to set a
boundary with another adult. It feels uncomfortable,
awkward even, which is why we are hesitant to do it.
Adults are supposed to know the basic rules and social
norms. Most do, but some adults either don't understand    h o w
the rules and norms change as children become adults, or they feel
that these rules and norms don't (or shouldn't) apply to them.

In the first case, adults will willingly abide by rules if they know
what they are; in the second case, these adults have learned that if
they ignore the basic rules and norms, they will get their way. People
do not like dealing with this kind of unpleasant person (particularly
when that person is not getting what they want), so they usually find
it's easier to give in to them. This suits the difficult person just fine.
People who don't abide by the rules and social norms have the greatest
impact when they are your in-laws, particularly your MIL.

Let me speak about these two different types of MILs, because
their reasoning for not following what seems like basic logic is quite
different, which means how you deal with them is also different. Let
me start with the MIL who doesn't realize that the rules change once
her child becomes an adult. As I detailed in *Reluctantly Related*, this
type of person is a Mothering Margaret. She truly does not want to
cause problems. She very much wants a relationship with her son, DIL,
and their children. She just hasn't figured out that her role has changed
significantly now that her son is a married adult.

Margaret is still trying to play a major role in the life of her son
and the rest of his family. She does not realize that she needs to take a
more secondary role. In all fairness though, as I mentioned in previous
chapters, she may have an intellectual understanding of this, but she
does not yet have the emotional awareness of what this means. This
integration is critical to Mothering Margaret understanding what her
son and his family need from her at this point in their lives.

The other type of MIL doesn't seem to care about social norms or what rules you set for her, because she is going to do whatever she wants anyway. In *Reluctantly Related*, she's the one I call Off-the-Wall Wanda. The reason Wanda is able to get her way so often is that most DILs feel awkward setting boundaries for her. Wanda's DILs are caught off guard by Wanda's actions or they're in shock because of them.

If Wanda is your MIL, you're often so uncomfortable with the situation at that moment that you tend to ignore her inappropriate behavior, hoping it's a fluke or just a misstep on her part. Or worse yet, you just don't *want* to deal with it because every time you've tried to set a boundary with her, she has trampled all over it. You feel exasperated, and for good reason! I cannot count the number of times DILs have told me, "I've tried setting boundaries with her, but when I do she either ignores me, defies me and does something just to spite me, or she flat out says she will do as she pleases because she's 'the mom.'"

A problem that often arises when you are dealing with an Off-the-Wall Wanda is that sometimes your husband doesn't seem to understand your frustration, hurt, and angst with his mother. It's not that he thinks his mother's behavior is appropriate—he doesn't—it's that he doesn't understand why you let it bother you. He doesn't get why you can't just ignore his mother's antics and take them for what they are—crazy behavior.

What your husband is forgetting is that he has grown up dealing with these antics. He's had years to learn how to maneuver around them, dodging and darting, avoiding and ignoring. He doesn't consider that you did not grow up with this kind of behavior and are not accustomed to it. He also doesn't realize that his chosen coping strategy may have worked well when he was a child and as he was growing up, but now that he is an adult, such avoidance behavior is not only ineffective, but also enables his mother to continue behaving in inappropriate ways.

Whether your MIL is a Mothering Margaret or an Off-the-Wall Wanda, you must learn to set boundaries with her so that you can get the relationship on track and keep it there. Boundary setting will also give you some peace of mind, allowing you to feel better about your relationship with your in-law. But how you set the boundaries depends on which type of MIL you have. What works for one will not work for the other.

Let's start with setting boundaries for a Mothering Margaret. Unlike an Off-the-Wall Wanda, Margaret is willing to abide by what you want—she just has to know what that is. So if you gently and kindly set a boundary with her, she will do her darnedest to give you what you want. For example, let's say she wants you and your husband to come over almost every weekend for a family dinner, and you find this too much family togetherness. You can easily set a boundary with her by casually saying in a compassionate tone, "We *love* having dinner with everyone, but we are finding it hard to get away so often. It would work better for us if we can plan on one definite family dinner a month, and then if we are able to come more often, we gladly will." Not only are you setting a boundary, but you are also coming up with a solution so that you have not left her with an all-or-nothing situation.

When you are dealing with an Off-the-Wall Wanda, however, you need a different approach. With Wanda, setting boundaries is not enough. You have to have consequences to go with the boundaries if you want the boundary setting to be effective.

Unlike Mothering Margaret, Wanda is not someone you can reason with or expect to understand your position. Because she's used to getting exactly what she wants, you have to set boundaries *with consequences*. Here are some things to consider when dealing with an Off-the-Wall Wanda:

- **Your goal is not getting your MIL to understand your position.** Remember with whom you are dealing. Off-the-Wall Wanda does not want to understand your position. She does not care about *why* you want her to do something differently. All she cares about is what she wants. This is all she can focus on.

- **When you set boundaries with consequences, make sure you do so in a kind, nonthreatening way.** When you do this, you are taking the focus off you and *how* you are saying what you're saying. Instead, you're keeping the focus on the boundary and the consequence. This assures that you will handle the situation in the best way possible. Most likely, Wanda will then try to make it seem as though she's a victim, but you won't have anything to apologize for because you won't be giving her a valid reason for playing the victim role. She will still feel like a victim, but you will have an easier time not buying into her act.

- **After you set the boundary, move on.** After you set your boundary and the consequence that will occur if your MIL does not abide by it, *do not get into a discussion, debate, or explanation or engage in any other way with her.* If you do, she will win! Once she gets you to start explaining yourself, she will have all her reasons why what you want is unreasonable, unfair, and so on. You do not have to, nor should you, give a reason for what you are asking of her. Remember, she is not asking why because she wants to know, she is asking why so she can challenge whatever you say in an attempt to get what she wants.

- **Be willing to follow through with the consequence you set.** You have to follow through with your consequences *each and every time*. Consistency is critical to the success of your MIL doing what you ask.

Yes, setting boundaries—not to mention setting boundaries with consequences—will feel awkward at first, whether you are setting a boundary for a Mothering Margaret or for an Off-the-Wall Wanda. That's okay. Feeling awkward or uncomfortable is a small price to pay for peace of mind and for gaining a sense of control over your situation with your MIL. And remember, particularly with an Off-the-Wall Wanda, *she* is the one putting you in the position of having to set these boundaries and these consequences. If she had healthy boundaries of her own, like most people, you would not have to set them for her.

## Guilt Trips

Guilt trips are something we are all familiar with, either because other people have guilt-tripped us or because we've guilt-tripped someone else. Depending on which side of this equation you have been on, you either view guilt trips as something that is just part of relationships (and a way to get what you want from another person) or you have a mix of emotions about them, ranging from being mildly uncomfortable to full-on resentful.

Guilt trips are a means of one person trying to control a second person's behavior and trying to get that person to do what the first person wants, with no regard to how the second person feels or what *they* may want. Sometimes these guilt trips seem innocent, as when a parent says to a small child, "You make Mommy *so* sad when you do that," or to an adult child, "Well, if you can't make it, then you can't. It's just been *so long* since we've seen you." Or it might be a wife saying to her husband, "You should know I can't stand it when your mother...." Regardless of who says it or how it's said, guilt trips are a way to manipulate or coerce this person you love into behaving the way you want.

Guilt trips definitely have a lasting impact on the receiver's well-being because in addition to guilt, they also create intense feelings of resentment. Even so, they are still effective because people use them on others who have a strong emotional investment in the guilt-tripper's happiness (such as a parent, child, spouse, or close friend).

Because of these strong feelings of caring and affection for the person who guilt-tripped you, you are able to override any resentment or anger that you have toward the person who is trying to manipulate you. Otherwise, the resentment would override any feelings of guilt you might have, rendering the technique useless. This is why your partner, who has less emotional attachment to your family, is not as affected as you are by any guilt trip your family may attempt to hook you with.

Even though you may love the person who is trying to make you feel guilty, these strong feelings of resentment do not just go away. In reality, the resentment gets stuffed down, buried deep within. As time goes on, the resentment piles up, causing you to emotionally detach and physically try to remove yourself from the presence of the guilt-tripper as much as possible. This creates a vicious cycle: You pull back, and when the other person gets frightened that you are going away, they guilt-trip you more; then you move closer to them briefly because of the guilt, before finally pulling back further because of the mounting resentment. And on it goes.

People who use guilt trips in their relationships do not consider the impact this action has on the person they love. Their focus is on the short term (getting what they want) and not on the long term (how their behavior is hurting their loved one—and ultimately damaging their relationship with them).

Guilt-trippers imply that if you really cared about them, you would see that what they are asking is the reasonable thing to do. Most of the time, they imply this not only in their actual words, but also in the *way* they say it, including their body language, tone of voice, and so on. They may say, for example, "If you really cared about me, you'd do this for me," "We used to be so close! I don't know what's happened," "If you were more understanding, you'd do what I'm asking," or "You don't care how I feel!"

People who use guilt trips will constantly test you. You may sometimes be successful at getting them to stop, but they will most likely try the same behavior again. And so you will need to keep your guard up and consistently refuse to buy into the guilt trip they try to put on you. No matter what they say or how often they say it, you will need to stand firm and not back down. If you back down *even once*, they will see that they can still get you to do what they want, and the cycle will begin anew.

## Action Steps

- Make a list of the kinds of things you do or say to your husband that may indicate the issues you are having are marital instead of being issues you have with your MIL.

- Reflect on what unrealistic expectations you may have of your husband when it comes to these MIL/DIL issues and how they affect your marriage.

- Decide what you need to do for yourself to make setting boundaries with your MIL (as well as setting any necessary consequences) easier for you.

- Evaluate how well you and your husband are working together to make boundary setting more effective.

- Ask yourself honestly if you guilt-trip your husband to get him to do what you want. If you do, think about how this behavior might affect your marriage in the long term.

- If you or your husband is the recipient of a guilt trip:
  - List the different trigger words or phrases that get you to feel guilty.
  - List how these triggers make you feel (and include *all* the different feelings).
  - Consider how you can turn these feelings around so that they empower you to act differently instead of cripple you into submission.

# CHAPTER 11

# Other In-Laws

*We come into families through the people we choose to marry. Our judgments about our in-laws speak more about who we are than who they are. Being mindful about what we bring to the situation helps create a well-balanced family environment.*

UP TO THIS POINT, we've been specifically focusing on the MIL/DIL relationship and on how the different people in the relationship affect it. I've also shared some ideas about the influence the MIL/DIL relationship has on other in-law relationships. But more affects the other in-law relationships than just the impact of the MIL/DIL relationship, as major an impact as that might have. So how do these other in-law relationships— fathers-in-law, sons-in-law, sisters-in-law, and brothers-in-law—affect one another? What can we learn about these relationships that might shed some light on the extended family dynamic—beyond the MIL/DIL relationship?

## Men vs. Women in the Family

Men and women behave quite differently in family relationships because they generally view relationships very differently. These differences, and the way they influence each person's behavior, can cause stress, strain, and even irreparable damage within the family—and they can also cause the marital partners to argue more about one or both extended families. This happens because the differences between how men and women see relationships are usually not clearly understood—by either party. As a rule, men focus on broad, more universal commonalities (things outside of themselves) when they interact with other family members. Women, however, focus more on specific commonalities, particularly how other people are emotionally affected by the relationship.

In other words, a man tends to focus on *activities* he may have in common with another person, such as sports, hobbies, cars, and music, as well as his work or profession. A man also seems to take these moments with family at face value. He spends little time, if any, judging, analyzing, or measuring what one particular in-law says or does with another family member. And as a result, a man typically does not feel competitive with other family members.

I'm not saying that a man always *likes* his in-laws; he may or may not. What I am saying is that he measures his thoughts, feelings, and opinions about any particular in-law based on how that in-law treats the other people in the family, particularly *his* spouse. Therefore, a man's personal feelings about any of his in-laws are usually based on their outward behavior and are not intertwined with his own internal conflicts or issues.

A woman, on the other hand, tends to focus more on the relationship itself and what similarities the other person has with her—as well as how the in-law meets (or doesn't meet) her emotional needs and how what the in-law says or does makes her feel. In other words, although women want to connect with others on some level—whether through personal interests, activities, or similarities in personality and values—the strongest criterion for forming a relationship is the need to connect on an emotional level. And of particular importance is how she *feels* the other person treats her.

Women take *all* their relationships personally. A woman needs to like a person based on who the person is, how that person treats her, and how that person befriends her. Rarely do women want to just be casual acquaintances with in-laws. A woman wants to matter in this newly created family system, and she wants the different family members to recognize *her* position in it (based on what she herself believes her position to be).

As a result, a woman can, and often does, feel threatened by other family members' perceived position in the family, particularly by an in-law's position or influence over *her* spouse or brother.

```
         DIL
        /\
       /  \
   HUSBAND\
   CHILDREN
   MOM - DAD
    SIBLINGS
   SIL & BIL
      FIL
     MIL
```

Such women who feel threatened constantly measure and judge who responds to whom, how they respond, and how these actions specifically impact her and her place or standing in the family. This internal monitoring occurs each and every time they are around family or whenever they interact with different family members one-on-one. Luckily, not all women are like this; some (including Comfortable Carla and Confident Connie as described in *Reluctantly Related*) never experience this type of perceived threat at all, and if they ever do, it's only as a fleeting thought.

Sibling relationships are one example of how male and female differences show themselves within the family. As a general rule, women who were close with their sisters growing up (and who remained close to them well into adulthood) have a very different experience than the men who were close to their brothers growing up. In my research, these women generally report observations such as, "Our husbands just seemed to go with the flow," or "They saw that we sisters were close, and they wanted to be a part of that too. We all get along great. Everyone seems to respect what we have in our family and wants to build on it."

These women and their husbands are able to take the closeness found among sisters and extend that to include their spouses. This inclusion makes for a stronger bond among the women because spouses are now a part of this inner circle. Much of this is due to how men view relationships and the fact that they do not feel threatened by the other family relationships nor do they feel the need to be competitive with their in-laws.

Men, on the other hand, seem to experience their sisters-in-law differently. In my research, I found that men were often frustrated with their sister-in-law and even sometimes with their brother because he allowed his wife to come between them. Many of the men report observations such as, "We used to be so close, but ever since he got married he's not allowed to even talk to me. His wife gets mad if I call him, often picking a fight with my wife or me just so she doesn't have to spend time with us." Many such men may add, "When we do get together, my sister-in-law makes it so difficult. Every chance she gets she picks a fight or lies about something I've supposedly said, just to stir the pot. Even my brother admits his wife doesn't like it when we get together, and yet he doesn't do anything about it."

In this example of the brothers who were close growing up, it is easy to see that the wives feel the need to compete with their husband's brother for the influence each one may have over him in much the same way that they compete with their MILs for influence over him. This need to compete is often present when a woman struggles within herself to feel of value and either doesn't trust or feel that she is the priority in her husband's life. In reality, though, she is taking a personal, internal conflict and turning it into a family and marital issue.

As you can see, men and women have differing views and perspectives on relationships in general, and especially on relationships within the family. These differences play out constantly within family dynamics and often cause family relationships to go awry. Let's look at some of these individual family members to see why they think and perceive the way they do and how they then respond within the family.

## Fathers-in-Law

A father-in-law is typically in the background more than anyone else when it comes to the different in-law relationships. He usually says little and doesn't react or step into situations. He shows up, interacts to the degree he is comfortable, and treats everyone basically the same. Whether he is happy or not with what he sees going on, he normally doesn't get overly emotional or overly involved. Therefore, most of the time the father-in-law is quiet, maybe passive, and definitely in the background—at least until there is an issue with his wife and one of their children or a child's spouse.

As we saw in an earlier chapter, men see one of their roles as a husband to be protector and "fixer." If a man's wife is hurt, angry, or frustrated, he feels the need to make things better for her. And yet this is a precarious position for a father-in-law. He watches what is going on between his wife (the MIL) and his son's wife (the DIL), and he watches what goes on between his wife and their son. And yet, as the MIL struggles with their DIL, the father-in-law often finds that his DIL does not have issues with *him*. In fact, many times she will converse with him and yet shun his wife. As a result, his wife feels even *more* hurt because of the obvious difference in how their DIL treats her compared with how she treats her husband. He, on the other hand, feels uncomfortable and awkward with the whole situation.

When the father-in-law sees how their DIL's words and behavior affect his wife, he doesn't know what to do. It is hard for him to watch his wife feel pain of any kind, especially emotional pain. When she struggles with their DIL or their son, he struggles too—not because he is impacted in the same way as his wife, but more because he feels helpless to fix something he cannot fix.

He does not view these situations with his son and DIL in the same way his wife does. He is baffled by what he sees each person doing to the other, and how his wife allows their DIL's words to have so much power. He also doesn't grasp why his wife cannot create some emotional distance to help her lessen the pain, or why their son deals with them (and particularly his mother) the way he does. Regardless of whether the father-in-law understands or not, he still can't bear to see his wife in pain, and it is at this point that he is likely to take action.

He may first use a less direct approach by talking to his wife to try to get her to brush things off, to not take things personally, or to pull back so she doesn't continue getting hurt. This often creates problems between the father-in-law and his wife. She sees his attempts to fix things as his lack of understanding her or her pain. For his part, though, he sees his actions as his attempt to at least try to do *something*.

When the MIL struggles with their son—when she gets scared or feels hurt, anger, or confused about his behavior—the father-in-law winces, often aching as he watches his wife struggle. He has his thoughts, opinions, and feelings about what he sees, but he mostly remains quiet—up to a point. After all, *this is his wife and their son at odds with one another.* Once he feels the line has been crossed, he will often step in and handle the situation the way he feels necessary to stop what he considers to be "the madness." After all, he feels a son should not disrespect his mother.

Yet the father-in-law still feels helpless, which brings to the surface his anger—anger about feeling helpless, anger about his inability to fix it, and anger about the fact that this situation is even happening in his family. This anger often erupts in one of two ways. He might take an "all-or-nothing" approach, where he feels that because the pain being caused is not worth it, it's better (or easier) to simply remove whoever is causing the pain from their lives altogether. Or he might speak out loudly and forcefully to the person causing the pain, saying whatever he feels is necessary to stop the insanity. Although neither approach creates the solution he hopes for, he is doing the best he can with what he knows. His reaction is as much about his own helplessness as it is about fixing the problem—and maybe more.

## Sons-in-Law

As I have said before, a man does not look at relationships in the same way as his wife does. This is particularly true when it comes to his view of the relationship between his wife and her mother versus his wife's view of the relationship between him and *his* mother. A DIL can, and often does, have difficulty with the relationship she sees between her husband and his mother, and she can then make that a point of contention between her and her husband. The same cannot be said of a son-in-law and his MIL. Women often feel that because their husband doesn't say anything about how often the couple sees or talks with her mother or about how much her mother may meddle in their marital affairs, that means he finds nothing wrong with what her mother says or does. This is not necessarily the case.

A husband often doesn't say anything because, as I said earlier, a man wants his wife to be happy. Her happiness means more to him than just about anything else. If seeing her mother as often as she does (or as often as they do as a couple) or if letting his MIL be involved in their life to a certain degree is what his wife wants, he will usually go along with it. Is he thrilled about it? Probably not. Does he think it is worth fighting over? Not really. But just because he doesn't say anything doesn't mean he is completely accepting of the situation. He may find that it is easier to just say nothing and deal with it. When he does try to say something, however, he will usually do so in a joking, off-handed manner because saying something too directly or too firmly will likely cause a fight between him and his wife. And the *last* thing he wants to do is fight with his wife.

A son-in-law's relationship with his father-in-law is often one of respect due to the father-in-law's role and position in the family, as well as a mutual "male understanding." Again, men understand what it means for a male to be a man and have his own family. Yes, you hear about the stereotypes of "no man is good enough for my little girl," but in reality, men tend to understand and accept each other in a way women don't grasp. For men it is more about, *If you treat my daughter well, provide for her, and make her happy, you are okay in my book*. Without it ever being stated, a son-in-law knows and respects this.

### Sisters-in-Law

Sisters-in-law have a common bond that only a sister-in-law can understand and appreciate—they married into this family and share the same MIL. When one or more of the DILs do not get along with the MIL, each one knows that there is at least one other person who understands what they are going through in their MIL/DIL relationship. She knows she has someone with whom she can share and commiserate. However, when this is the only tie that bonds the sisters-in-law, the need to maintain the MIL/DIL strife is high, making for a fragile and weak sister-in-law relationship. At any moment there can be a shift from one or the other, altering whatever connection the two of them once had.

When a sister-in-law does not feel comfortable in her own skin or confident about who she is (or worse, if they both feel that way), the relationship between sisters-in-law can become competitive. As one struggles with the MIL, the other can use that strained relationship to get in good graces with her MIL. This causes a triangulation between the MIL and the sisters-in-law. The "good" sister-in-law, by playing up to her MIL, validates the MIL's perceptions, pointing out unacceptable behaviors by the other "bad" sister-in-law, giving her opinions about that sister-in-law, and so on—all to keep the drama and tension going between their MIL and the other sister-in-law.

The competitiveness can also come out when a sister-in-law feels she doesn't have the same power or position in the family as another sister-in-law. In these situations, everything is personal between the women. Too often, they measure, judge, and analyze every word, behavior, and nuance displayed by the other. Their strained relationship can, and often does, spill over into the sibling relationship as well, adding to the stress, strain, and drama in the family. For example, one or both may not want to have anything to do with the other and will want their spouse to follow suit, will refuse to attend family gatherings if the other one is going to be present, or will refuse to work out the issues with the other.

What about the husband's sister who is also a sister-in-law? This relationship—the DIL and her husband's sister—can often be strained because, like with other females, they are characteristically competitive for the influence each one has over the husband/brother. Along with this the sister-in-law is also the daughter of the MIL. The allegiance she has is likely with her mother (the MIL), leaving her sister-in-law feeling like an outsider.

## Brothers-in-Law

Like the other males in the family, brothers-in-law remain as neutral as possible when it comes to the family dynamics. When a man's wife and her siblings get along, he will make an effort to get along with them as well. Unlike sisters-in-law who sometimes form a bond with one other, making their relationship separate from that of her husband's relationship with his sister or her relationship with her brothers, a brother-in-law doesn't typically create a separate relationship with a sister-in-law. He may be pleasant, talk with her about things they have in common (such as kids, work, his wife, and so on). But often that is where it stops. He may be more inclined to develop some kind of relationship with his wife's brother or brothers or his sister's husband, but only if they have things in common. A brother-in-law does not feel compelled to create a relationship, other than a friendly one, with another in-law. As you might expect, the gender difference is behind this. Again, men tend to focus on bonding over activities whereas women bond over emotional connections.

In all situations, though, a man is keenly aware of how his in-laws treat his wife, and this becomes the major factor affecting how he relates to other family members. When they treat her well, he is affable and responsive toward them. If he feels his wife is being treated badly by one or more of them, he is likely to speak up as a way to protect or defend her.

## Ideal Family Relationships

With so much going on in these family relationships, it seems almost impossible to believe that *some* families actually get along just fine. How can that be when everyone comes into this extended family situation with so many of their own issues and emotional baggage, as well as their own family history, traditions, ways of communicating, and so on? Just as with the MIL/DIL relationship, the family as a whole *can* get along well. But again, it's not by magic. Here are some of the characteristics that help in-laws get along with one another (as long as each person plays their part):

- Everyone feels comfortable in their own skin.

- Family members have at least some things in common.

- Siblings are close or have addressed any latent baggage between them.

- Siblings show respect toward one another (which carries over to the in-laws).

- Everyone allows each person the space to make mistakes and not be perfect.

- Each person allows for differences between each other.

- In-laws let go—they don't hold on to things other family members may say or do.

- The in-law treats their spouse well—and other siblings see this, making them feel respectful of the spouse.

- In-law are good to the other siblings' children.

- Mothers-in-law and fathers-in-law are respectful of their children and are appreciated and respected by their children.

Unlike MIL/DIL relationships that struggle, brothers-in-law and sisters-in-law who feel less than thrilled to spend time together are able to keep their distance from the offensive party most of the time. If these in-laws have to come together for a family gathering, they can do so with less anxiety and pressure because these interactions are often few and far between. This is why many sisters-in-law and brothers-in-law do not feel the need to work on their relationship with one another.

MILs and DILs, on the other hand, are in a different position with one another. These two women have such high stakes—marriage, son, and children/grandchildren—and they are likely to interact frequently. The consequences for not getting along are paramount and affect not only the two of them and the marital status, but also the other members of the family.

## Action Steps

- Describe in detail how your husband views relationships differently than you do.

- As you focus on these different viewpoints, reflect on the ways you can use these insights about his perspective to make your relationships better.

- Identify how you let your spouse know your expectations and desires. Be specific. Answer the following questions:

  o How could you make your expectations clearer to him?

  o How do you handle the situation when expectations aren't clear?

  o What is your role in the communication struggle between you and your spouse, and what could you do differently to make this communication better?

# CHAPTER 12

# Beyond the MIL/DIL Relationship

*Many people in your life behave similarly to the MILs and DILs in this book. As with MILs and DILs, when you know which type of person they are, you will know how to respond to them. This gives you the power to change any relationship for the better.*

NOW THAT YOU HAVE A BETTER UNDERSTANDING of the MIL/DIL relationship and how it affects other in-law relationships—not to mention the dynamics of the other in-law relationships in general—you probably see a connection between some of these different types of people and others in your life. After all, there are a few other categories of family members with whom you may also feel reluctantly related, such as stepparents and stepsiblings. And if you are really honest, these types of struggles that have you feeling "reluctantly related" can include the relationships you have with your mother and your sisters as well.

Family members aside, there are also people you are *not* related to—such as coworkers and friends—with whom you might also feel "stuck" in a relationship. You may find it easier to maneuver around these peripheral relationships because you either don't interact with these people on a daily basis or (particularly with coworkers) you don't view the relationships as personal. But you still have to deal with these people on some basis. Friends, of course, you can generally choose to keep in your life or not. However, we sometimes stay in friendships that aren't always comfortable because we convince ourselves that we're around these people for only short periods of time and we get enough out of the relationship that it's worth some discomfort to keep it going.

Throughout both this book as well as throughout *Reluctantly Related,* I have described MILs and DILs with specific characteristics and behaviors. These distinctive qualities, however, are not limited to MILs and DILs. Each specific personality that I've talked about previously can apply to other people in your life, as well.

Consider these stories about some similar relationship issues and see if any of these characters sound familiar:

Paula can't believe this was happening *again!* All she wants to do is spend time with her dad, and yet every time she tries to see him, he says that he is doing something with his wife Clara's family or that Clara has them off doing something together. Sometimes Paula doesn't even get a chance to talk with him on the phone because Clara says he isn't available when she calls.

Clara and Paula's dad have been married five years—they married just a year after Paula's mother died. Initially, Clara was pleasant and even friendly toward Paula. But as that first year moved into the second, she started to change—and so did Paula's dad. Thinking back, Paula didn't realize that her father was becoming less accessible at the time because it happened so gradually. But now, after five years, she rarely gets to see her dad, and when she does, it seems that Clara won't ever leave the two of them alone together. She seems to always be *right there*!

Paula has tried talking to her dad about it, but that's a challenge because Clara makes it almost impossible for them to talk openly. She also tried to talk with Clara, hoping she could reason with her. "Clara, I just want to spend some time with my dad. Isn't there some way we can make that happen?" she'd asked hopefully.

"You think you're being so clever, don't you?" Clara had sneered in response. "I know what you're up to. You've never liked the fact that your father married me, and now you think you can come between us. I won't let you do that! Your father knows what you're up to as well, believe me!" It was bad enough that Clara had challenged Paula's motives, but then she had also started telling Paula's dad lies about her.

Paula's tensions with her stepmother are causing her relationship with her father to deteriorate right in front of her eyes, and she feels helpless to stop her stepmother from completely removing him from Paula's life. She feels she cannot fight the distortions, lies, and misrepresentations about her that her stepmother is feeding her father and putting out there to the world. And as if that wasn't bad enough, Paula's young daughter Stephanie feels hurt and confused by what she sees as her once-loving grandfather pushing her and her mother away. That alone is enough to break Paula's heart. *Stepmother?* Paula thinks. *Ha! Clara is more like a step-monster!*

Nan is at her wit's end. Never before has she experienced such insubordination! She realizes she is fairly new to this supervisory role, but she has, at least up to this point, had a very good track record for getting people to work up to and beyond their potential. She has always taken pride in her ability to work with people and to get people to work with her. However, that has all changed now that Tim and Kay have come to work for her.

Nan has been at her company for more than eight years, but she's been in her current position for only a year and a half. She worked her way up the corporate ladder to a highly visible supervisory position. She currently manages ten people at various levels of talent, creativity, and proficiency, in a department where people have generally been cooperative and supportive. All that has changed now.

Tim and Kay have seen to that. They seem to feed off each other's ability to buck the system. Showing disrespect to colleagues is bad enough, but they're also disrespectful of Nan. This not only affects the morale of her coworkers, but it also undermines Nan's authority with the group. Consequently, productivity and morale are taking a nosedive. Being late to meetings, blaming others in the group when things don't go smoothly, and missing deadlines that then put other group members' assignments at risk are only some of the antics Tim and Kay seem to specialize in.

Nan has talked to both Tim and Kay on numerous occasions, but they always have an excuse for their behavior. They always give some reason for why their actions are justifiable—to *them.* Although their offenses aren't quite overt enough to warrant Nan firing them, she can't help ruminating on one agonizing fear: *The effect these two are having on the department might be bad enough to get* me *fired!*

## Setting Strong Boundaries

In both of these scenarios, we are not talking about a MIL or DIL, but instead, about people who create just as much stress, tension, and havoc for everyone around them. Both Paula and Nan feel helpless in their situations, not knowing what to do to turn things around. They keep trying over and over to get the offending characters to change, sure that if they could only figure out what to do, it would make things better for everyone.

Paula and Nan feel everything that an in-law can feel when she is dealing with an MIL or DIL who is either unwilling or unable to address the issues—and who is certainly unwilling to meet her halfway. And not only is the behavior of these "problem people" affecting Paula and Nan, but it's also having a negative impact on those around them.

It is easy to dismiss the people who are causing you so much angst with, "She's just crazy," or "I just try to avoid her as much as possible," but in reality, you can't always avoid them. And in the end, you are still—at some point or another—going to have to deal with the impact they have on you. However, if you understand the type of person you are dealing with and if you apply the same principles to them that you have learned about the different types of MILs and DILs, you can begin to change these relationships, as well.

Let's take Nan's experience with her staff members as an example. If you look at the behaviors that both Tim and Kay display, you begin to see a pattern. Their actions look a lot like an Off-the-Wall Wanda—a disregard for rules, doing whatever they want at the expense of others, total disregard for how they impact others, and so on. As with an Off-the-Wall Wanda, setting boundaries with consequences is critical to changing behavior and getting the results you want. Setting boundaries with consequences is also necessary for Nan in dealing with Tim and Kay.

Once Nan understands with whom she is dealing, she is able to see that reasoning with them or getting either of them to "understand" is not only not possible, but it's also not necessary. All she needs from Tim and Kay is a change in their behavior. Here's what happened:

Nan sent out a memo to all of her staff that said, "Effective immediately, weekly staff meetings are scheduled for Mondays at 10 a.m. The door will be shut at that time and the meetings will start promptly. Because these meetings are critical to the congruency of our group as well as our productivity, anyone not in the room by 10 a.m. will not be allowed to join the meeting. All information discussed in these meetings will be available only to those people participating in them. Further, missing the meeting will be documented and this documentation will be placed in your file."

This memo was the first step Nan took to set healthy boundaries. The next step was following through with the consequences. When Nan followed through with shutting the door and not letting anyone enter who tried to do so after 10 a.m., she provided the stated consequence. Because everyone was given the memo in advance, no one could say, "I didn't know."

Tim and Kay responded just like anyone who is guilty of challenging authority usually would—by resorting to whatever manipulative behavior they've used in the past to exempt themselves from the consequences. (After all, it has worked in the past!) They knocked on the door, made excuses as to why they were late, and tried to blame others for their tardiness. Nan stood firm. And when she did so, it was only a matter of time before Tim and Kay stopped violating the boundary—coming to the meeting late—and started arriving on time.

As with an Off-the-Wall Wanda, the key to effective boundary setting is following through each and every time with setting the boundary *and* with enforcing the consequence. Further, you cannot engage the person in any form of discussion, debate, or rationalization of your actions. The minute you engage with them, they win. Whether they know this consciously or unconsciously, they sense that if they can engage you, they have a chance to wear you down. And just as with an Off-the-Wall Wanda, this is their goal—they want what they want. However, you *don't* have to accept this type of behavior, and you *do* have the power to help them change it.

## Strategic Responses

What about Paula and her stepmother Clara? Again, if you look at Clara's behavior, you can start to see a pattern that looks a lot like the DIL character Weird Wendy. The distortions and manipulative behavior make dealing with someone like this extremely difficult, but (as in the case of Weird Wendy) not impossible. Two facets will likely come into play here: how she affects you in the moment and how her actions impact you overall.

Let me start with how Clara impacts Paula in the moment. Usually, Clara's egregious words or actions leave Paula speechless and often positively seething. She is racked with such internal turmoil at what Clara did or said that she not only doesn't know how to respond, but she also completely forgets *to* respond. Because no one can anticipate every possible scenario that a Weird Wendy will present, it is imperative to store some responses "in your back pocket."

One such standard response to a Weird Wendy saying something outrageous might be to utter a generic, *"Really?"* or to ask an innocent, confused, did-I-just-hear-you-right type of question. Whatever you choose, these generic responses allow you to make a point without having to directly confront the other person, since doing so will get you nowhere except in a shouting match with her. Another approach is to use laughter. Not the kind of laughter that makes it seem that you are making fun of her, but instead the oh-you-are-so-funny kind of laugh. (You can read a detailed version of these different approaches in *Reluctantly Related*.)

Paula can use these tactics to handle those moments when she is caught off guard, but what about the overall impact of Clara's distortions and manipulative behavior? Again, taking a cue from the advice for handling a Weird Wendy, Paula will find it easiest if she "helps" Clara with those distortions or manipulative behaviors. The best way to do that is by mirroring her words back to her.

Here's an example:

Paula noticed that every time Clara made one of her nasty remarks to Paula, her father was never around. And later when she would say something to her father about what Clara had said to her, he just couldn't believe Clara would say anything like that. This was not only maddening to Paula, but it also made her feel helpless. How could she get her father to see what was going on, or at least get Clara to stop her vilifying remarks?

Paula developed a plan. She knew that it would take more than one try to change Clara's behavior, but Paula was on a mission. She made a pact with herself that she would be consistent with her plan. *Every* time Clara made one of those comments to Paula, Paula would mirror it back to Clara as though it had confused her and she wanted to either get clarification or at least make sure she heard it correctly. It didn't take long before Paula had her chance.

Paula had been trying to stop over to see her dad for more than a week. Every time she called to see if they were home and if it was a good time to stop by, Clara told her, "No, we're going out," or "It's not a good time. Your dad is resting." Paula was out running errands when she saw her dad and Clara walking into the store she just happened to be shopping in. She immediately went up to her father, gave him a big hug, and said, "Dad, I've been wanting to stop by but it seems you've either been so busy or you've been resting every time I've called to set something up."

"No, I haven't," her dad immediately responded. "I've been home, pretty much doing nothing."

Paula knew this was her chance. "Really? I must have misunderstood you, Clara, when you told me Dad was resting or that you guys were on your way out," she said as innocently as possible, with no sarcasm. "Do you think that's what happened, Clara? Well anyway, this is great seeing you! Now that we're all here, why don't we make a date to get together? What works for you two?"

Paula continued to use this strategy each and every opportunity she could, tailoring it to fit Clara's antics and whatever was happening at the moment. Although it took a while, she eventually was able to shift the barrier Clara had erected in front of her. She and Clara may never have the best of relationships, but Paula is at least able to see her dad more often, and Clara is not able to be as manipulative as she had been in the past. Paula feels proud of both how she handled things with Clara *and* the outcome.

As you can see in both of these situations, the person with whom you struggle does not have to be a MIL or DIL. And yet, you can see how their personalities are similar to those of the MILs and DILs that I've described. It's the *personality types* that are the key, as these various types are not exclusive to MILs and DILs. It is just a matter of paying attention to how people behave and how they impact you and others. You can use some of the other strategies and concepts (such as understanding the impact of perception and reaction, breaking a stalemate, understanding passive-aggressive behavior, and so on) in both this book and in *Reluctantly Related* to help you with these relationships, as well.

## Action Steps

- Make a list of the other people in your life with whom you struggle or feel "stuck."

- Go through the information you've worked with in this book, and compare the behaviors of the people on your list with the behavioral patterns previously outlined. Then identify which personality type each of those people most resembles.

- Read what you can about each of those personality types, paying special attention to the tools and strategies you can use to help change those relationships for the better.

- Create a plan of action for using these tools and strategies for each person on your list. Don't get discouraged if you don't succeed the first time you try to use the plan. Remember that changing how you respond is not easy and will take some practice. Count even small successes as victories that are getting you one step closer to you goal.

# The Characters
## MILs, DILs, and Husbands/Sons

### Mothers-in-Law

**Comfortable Carla**—She has created a new identity for herself beyond that of "mother." She is clear that her new role in her son's life is secondary to his wife's role.

**Mothering Margaret**—She struggles with letting go of her mom role. She wants things to be as they have always been, even though circumstances are now different.

**Off-the-Wall Wanda**—She comes across as mean, insensitive, and self-centered. Everything is about her and what she feels, wants, and needs. Her behavior is often extreme in nature.

**Uncertain Sara**—She has let go of her son, but she is uncertain about her new role as a mother to an adult child and to a DIL. Sometimes she tries too hard and sometimes she just misses the mark.

### Daughters-in-Law

**Confidant Connie**—She has a strong sense of who she is. She trusts herself, her thoughts, and her opinions. She likes who she is and sees herself as others see her.

**Doubting Donna**—She is not comfortable with who she is. She tends to second-guess her thoughts, feelings, and actions. More often than not, she is judgmental and self-critical.

**Weird Wendy**—She has little or no desire to engage with most people. As a result, she comes across as distant and aloof. She typically perceives any friends, family, or in-laws through distorted filters.

**Transitioned Tracy**—She has worked through earlier issues she had with her mother. She now feels comfortable with who she is and is fairly self-contained. She is independent and does not rely on others.

## Husbands/Sons

**Self-Assured Andy**—He is self-confident with a strong sense of who he is as a man. He stands firm on his beliefs and is comfortable with his role in life. He has established healthy boundaries with his mother.

**In-the-Middle Michael**—He feels caught in the middle between his wife and mother. He is not sure how to balance his relationship with each of them or where everyone fits in his new world as a man.

**Struggling Steven**—He is fairly okay with who he is, but not completely. He tends to overthink, over worry, and overanalyze his actions and their impact on other people.

# Resources

If you are interested in more information and resources, please visit www.DrDeannaBrann.com, where you can ask questions, get answers, and learn more about the MIL/DIL relationship. You will also find the following resources there:

- Information on ordering Dr. Brann's other books:
  - *Reluctantly Related: Secrets to Getting Along with Your Mother-in-Law or Daughter-in-Law*
  - *Mothers-in-Law & Daughters-in-Law Say the Darndest Things*
- One-on-one coaching or consulting opportunities
- Videos
- Download packages that include audio/video tutorials, action guides, PDFs, and more
- Information on booking Dr. Brann as a speaker

If you do not find what you need in these resources or if you are not sure which resource would be the best for you and your situation, please email Dr. Brann at Deanna@DrDeannaBrann.com.

*Remember, as much as we feel it is too late to change this relationship with our in-law—it isn't. The first step is a willingness to try.*

# About the Author

Deanna Brann, Ph.D., author of the award-winning *Reluctantly Related: Secrets to Getting Along with Your Mother-in-Law or Daughter-in-Law*, is the leading expert on mother-in-law/daughter-in-law relationships. Her expertise in this field has also garnered her national media recognition from ABC News, *Chicago Tribune*, *New York Post*, *Brides Magazine*, *Women's Day*, *Real Simple*, *Glamour*, *Huffington Post*, and AARP, to name a few who have asked her for clarity and guidance on maneuvering through this challenging, yet fragile relationship. Further, Dr. Brann continues to be highly sought both nationally and internationally by women who struggle in the mother-in-law/daughter-in-law relationship for assistance in creating a better and more enjoyable relationship.

Dr. Brann holds a Master of Science degree in clinical psychology and a Ph.D. in psychobiological anthropology, and she is a licensed clinical psychotherapist. She has worked in the mental health field for more than 30 years, spending 20 of those years as a private practitioner providing individual, marital, and family therapy. She's been a mother-in-law for more than 20 years and a daughter-in-law for more than 17 years.

Through her one-on-one coaching, seminars, and download packages, Dr. Brann teaches mothers-in-law and daughters-in-law the techniques for shifting their thinking to a new level, inspiring powerful insights that help them change their in-law relationship for the better—forever.

Dr. Brann is also the author of a cartoon book on mother-in-law/daughter-in-law relationships, with another one coming out soon. She maintains an interactive website, www.DrDeannaBrann.com, that specifically addresses mother-in-law/daughter-in-law issues.

Lightning Source UK Ltd.
Milton Keynes UK
UKOW05f1806191216
290411UK00019B/258/P